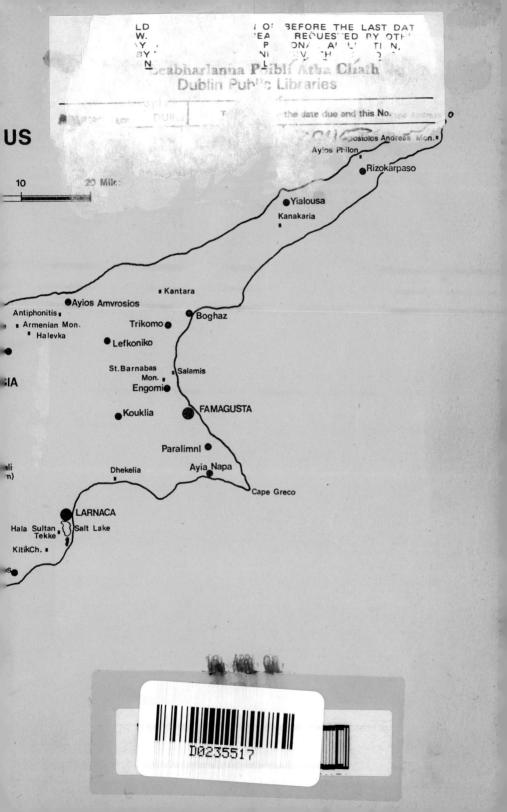

CYPRUS INVITATION

Cyprus Invitation

WILLIAM FORWOOD

Garnstone Press

Cyprus Invitation
is published by
GARNSTONE PRESS LIMITED
59 *Brompton Road, London* s.w.3
ISBN: 0 900391 53 7

© William Forwood 1971
Printed by A. Wheaton & Co., Exeter

CONTENTS

5

6

ILLUSTRATIONS

The author accepted an invitation to Cyprus and wishes to record his gratitude to the people of the island by dedicating this book to them

He is indebted to Spiros Phylaktis, Savvas Patsalides and Platon Christodoulides for all manner of assistance

To Peter Stylianakis, Burhan Garip, Konstantinos Kollis and David Winfield for their advice

To vintners and lemon planters, curators and excavators, students and soldiers, monks and birdcatchers

To people of the countryside and people of the *kafeneion* for diverse ideas

CHAPTER ONE

Cyprus Present

Geographic location – Topography – Climate – Accessibility –
Internal Transport – Tourism – Hotels – Food and wine –
Economic outline – Festivals – Particular attractions of the
Island's regions

Sprawled across their ancient hills, Athens and Piraeus retreat
into the deeper shades of evening. Lycabettus and the Acropolis are soon level with the Athenian coast. Yachts repose
like replicas in the holiday harbours and a score of steamers
swarm homewards across the Saronic Gulf to the sculpted
peaks of Argos and Aegina. Swiftly the islets of the Cyclades
are swallowed up by the night. The aircraft is bound for
Cyprus and the crew spread *mezedakia* and the sensuous
wines of Limassol before the traveller. Rhodes hides beneath
an isolated bank of cloud and we fly another hour till electric
lights again pinpoint the darkness. These are the westerly
beacons of Cyprus. The moon hangs high above the sharp
demarcations of a mountainous island and the sky is pricked
with stars. The aircraft circles over Nicosia and the swinging
landscape is suddenly stationary. Emotional welcomes extend
to returning kinsfolk : "Yanni ! Kosta !" Snatches of *hassapiko*
from the radio, and a drone of cicadas in the trees form a
desultory reception committee at journey's end.

A first visit to Cyprus is full of promise : island of the
Crusaders, of Aphrodite, of cypresses, of a perpetual Cythera

inhabited by an antique people. It raises questions. Is this another Majorca or Corfu spoiled by mass tourism? Are visiting tourists, particularly from Britain, at a disadvantage so soon after the Troubles of the 1950's? Will foreigners as a whole be put out by the recurrence of Graeco-Turkish conflict? The answers to such questions are oddly felicitous, as we shall see.

The island of Cyprus (*Kypros* in Greek, *Kibris* in Turkish) is geographically an annex of Asia Minor and culturally the easternmost of the Greek isles. Of Mediterranean islands, only Sicily and Sardinia are bigger, and Cyprus has the area of Norfolk and Suffolk combined, or of Puerto Rico. In shape resembling a fleece, a Georgian tea-pot or Aladdin's lamp, Cyprus is 140 miles from east to west, 60 miles at its bulge, 45 miles from the Turkish mainland and, from where the Karpas Peninsula points an accusing finger at the Syrian seaboard, 68 miles to the Middle East. Possessing nearly 500 miles of coast and an astonishing variety of landforms Cyprus is a country in its own right. The mountain people are a far cry from the peninsular folk of the east. Nicosians and Famagustans, like Milanese and Romans, dwell on their distinctions.

Cyprus has two mountain ranges: the spiny Kyrenia Mountains in the north—a limestone chain rising to more than 3000 feet – and the distinctive Troodos in the centre and south-west, a chunky massif of volcanic origin, reaching more than 6000 feet. Between these elevations a middle plain or Mesaoria is broken up in bare tablelands, while in the south, plateaux of snow-white marl and chalk march downwards to the sea. The northern coast, from Cape Kormakiti to the Karpas, is a fretwork of small, sandy and rocky inlets. Around the rest of the island a row of promontories: Cape Akamas, Kokkina Point, Capes Kormakiti, Andreas, Greco and Gata, divide one elliptical bay from another, lending coastal Cyprus as strong a particularity as the interior. There are places which call to mind not only Crete and Sicily but Cornwall, Sussex and Switzerland too. Changes in topography are matched in vegetation; Alpine flowers cohabit an island with bamboo and bananas, and man has on all sides imprinted the patterns of his cultivation. Crops and natural greenery are of course dependent on water and this is partly a matter of altitude. In summertime the Salt Lakes at Larnaca and Limassol evaporate into salt-pans and in the plain the fitful torrents of winter, often bridged by a mason's arabesques, are transformed into arid beds of stone.

Summer temperatures at Nicosia can intimidate but one should not forget the alleviating climate of the hills or the coast. Winter rain over the Troodos is nearly twice as heavy as on the Mesaoria; above a certain height the snow lingers till April and the ski-slopes of Troodos, Platres and Prodhromos draw winter sportsmen from all parts of the Near East. Then from May till the return of winter, the woods of the higher Troodos are watered by cool and tinkling streams. If in high August the Nicosia thermometer hovers above 90° the air comes whispering through the grey olive trees and carobs and we know that half an hour away at the seashore, the *livas* – a blustering summer wind like the Greek *meltemi* – churns the sea and fans the shore of Cyprus. Air-conditioning has come to stay and its pre-electric beginnings are in classical Paphos when doves, sacred to Aphrodite, were taught to flutter about the head of a Paphiot king, thus cooling his face. The Cyprian sea is forever warm, never dropping below 62°, and the longevity of Cypriots is as good proof as the barometer that the island's weather is milder than that of Sicily, Spain or mainland Greece. Its little seaports bathe for most of the year in the radiance of an eastern riviera. Lemons bloom twice and a kaleidoscope of wildflowers shifts in colour with the calendar; in spring especially the multitudes of crocuses, cyclamens, orchids and asphodels exorcise the northerner's wintry spirits and reveal the muse./

Cyprus is directly accessible by water from most ports of the Mediterranean, Aegean, Adriatic and Black Seas, and is linked more tenuously with northern Europe and the Americas. Few tourists today travel by boat, except as part of the Grand Tour to the Aegean, Holy Land and Egypt, but there is every advantage, apart from speed, in making the traditional sea voyage from Venice, from Piraeus or Istanbul, sailing in the wake of the Argonauts and Crusaders and edging breathlessly along the island's southern lee into the becalmed harbours of Limassol, Larnaca and Famagusta. The majority of travellers now arrive by air at Nicosia, which has direct links with a score of cities in Europe and the Near East. The flights from London to Nicosia are daily and are a contrast to the first ones made in 1930 by Imperial Airways, whose flying-boats operated a Palestinian route to the Lake of Galilee via the Akrotiri Salt Lake. The popular package holidays of today, arranged by several travel agencies and airlines in western Europe, make Cyprus far less expensive a proposition than the mileage would suggest.

As for journeys within the island, these are very simple to arrange. There are no railways, but the road system, already excellent, is ever being improved. In the eastern Mediterranean Cyprus is second only to Italy in the density of roads per square mile. Every point in the island is within an easy day's ride, and even from the remotest village of the Akamas or Karpas peninsulas, a return journey can be taken without qualms, in starlight and on roads beautifully free of traffic. There are three ways of travelling. Buses run on most routes and, like mumbling bees in search of wayside pollen, stop wherever a hand is raised. Popular as they are with the peasantry, their hours of operation are adjusted to the work timetable, thus confirming the Cypriot maxim : Early on the road and early home. Then there are "collective" taxis, reservable from any hotel at a rate of approximately 4 shillings for 25 miles. A forty-mile journey, as from Nicosia to Famagusta, will cost no more than 8 shillings, a bargain especially if the vehicle happens to be a brand-new Mercedes. Finally there is

Country Road

The Roman theatre at Curium

Turkish fortress guarding Paphos harbour

the self-drive car which is patently the best ally of every traveller who values independence. Such cars are available in all towns and resorts, either directly or through hotels, and will cost £2 or £3 a day, or relatively less for longer periods. Many of the island's finest and rarest attractions are well outside the towns and should be savoured at leisure. Thus the justification for a rented automobile.

Philoxenia or the law of hospitality to the stranger is still respected by the Cypriot; his courtesy is proverbial and it is instructive to read the comments made by the explorer Sir Samuel Baker, who travelled in Cyprus one century ago. "Although the crowd was large," he writes, "and all were busied in filling their jars and loading their respective animals, there was no jostling or quarrelling for precedence, but every individual was a pattern of patience and good humour. Mohammedans and Cypriots thronged together in the same employments, and the orderly behaviour in the absence of police supervision formed a strong contrast to the crowds in England."

The distant image of Cyprus perceived as is unhappily so often the case, through a haze of sensationalism in the aftermath of the 1950's, is today distorted—as virtually every visitor will judge for himself. Both official and personal relationships between Cyprus on the one hand and Britain on the other are again warmly cordial and the so-called Troubles were an anomaly in six hundred years of contact between England and Cyprus. Most Cypriots, whether Greek or Turkish, are Anglophile and even the memoirs of General Grivas speak of his love-hatred for the English. Scarcely a Cypriot does not claim kinsmen or friends living in Bristol or Camden Town. By 1969 over a hundred thousand Britons were visiting Cyprus, out-numbering the Americans, Greeks, Lebanese, Israelis, Germans, French and Swedes who were next in line. The two British sovereign bases, at Akrotiri and Dhekelia, support eight thousand servicemen together with their families, while UNFICYP (United Nations Forces in

Cyprus) has a further British contingent in a multinational force composed otherwise of Austrians, Australians, Canadians, Danes, Finns, Irish and Swedes. The leafy environs of Kyrenia and Famagusta are still colonised by Anglo-Saxons, mainly retired and drawn by lifelong loyalties to Cyprus as well as by the more obvious climatic attraction. British and American economic interests in Cyprus are lively and Great Britain remains, through habit and Commonwealth preference, the island's chief trading partner by a wide margin. The English language is not only an official medium but is understood by most townspeople and by the more worldly villager. Rather than scour out the cold statistics of broadcasting hours in English or dissect the budget of the sovereign bases (which earn £14 million a year), the observer will discern, not without amusement, other signs of the English presence: the Orthodox priest at the wheel of a Mini Morris – his mitre hitting the roof at every rise; the Cypriot society woman leafing through the pages of *Somerset Life*; the Jaeger styles of a Nicosia boutique; the VR pillar-boxes now painted in a splash of southern yellow; elderly Englishwomen with bobbed hair – caricatures of their imperial forebears – who pursue the guide at Famagusta in quest of the real Othello.

If the Anglo-Saxon does not feel already at home, the daily *Cyprus Mail* covers world and Cypriot news while the (Greek) *Cyprus Bulletin* and (Turkish) *News Bulletin* echo, in English, the official opinion of the two communities. Even the Greek newspapers record the results of British football. This is not to say that the two island races have everything in common; indeed it is the persistence of an intrinsically Greek culture which has given Cyprus an immunity from total absorption by the foreign overlords who determined the island's political history till independence. Cyprus, like Malta, has assimilated foreign influences by adaptation to local needs and tradition. From the Phoenician origins of the Aphrodite myth, from the Persian and Hittite impact on early Cypriot art, from the

Damascus goat and Aleppo pines of the countryside to the monuments of Franks and Venetians, to Turkish dress and gastronomy and the British heritage of a sterling currency and left-hand driving, the island has guarded its essential personality. If today they are playing bossa nova in the night bars and Irish tanks rumble incongruously through a remote hill village, if German business men bound for Israel take time off at Golden Sands, if one more London film-maker sets his cameras on the battlements of Kolossi it is certain that tomorrow's Cyprus will stay itself. Cultural continuity is an underlying theme of subsequent chapters.

Cyprus can thus benefit from the increasing revenues and foreign prestige of tourism, and the Government has in the last five years spared neither effort nor expense to improve the island's facilities. Cyprus Tourist Centres are now established in London (see Chapter 11 for addresses) and in Frankfurt-am-Main, and there are tourist departments in the Embassies of Cyprus at Washington, Paris and Cairo. In Nicosia both the Cyprus Government Tourist Office (at the Ministry of Commerce and Industry) and the Tourist Information Bureau (26 Evagoras Avenue) dispense advice and literature, as do similar offices in Famagusta, Limassol, Larnaca and Paphos. (See page 156.)

Till lately the demand for hotel accommodation exceeded supply but there are now several new hotels a-building, and long-term projects include a large hotel at Paphos (an Anglo-Cypriot venture), another near the idyllic Coral Bay (sponsored by Kykko Monastery), a holiday complex at Ayios Amvrosios (a quiet retreat on the north coast); a new village called Ambelia above the abbey at Bellapais, several youth-hostels, tourist pavilions and a network of broad highways linking Nicosia with the mountain resorts. In 1968 the Department of Planning and Housing drew up a master plan to safeguard the island's natural beauty. "Clusters" rather than conurbations are to be the rule; what Doxiades has done for Crete and the Aegean Islands will reappear in Cyprus, counteracting the ribbon growth which has threatened Kyrenia and Famagusta.

All towns and some villages have accommodation but the island's best hotels are located in Nicosia, in the beach areas of Famagusta and Limassol, on the Kyrenia coast and in the resorts of the Troodos Mountains. In *Nicosia* the first categories of hotel include the Ledra Palace, Cyprus Hilton, Regina Palace and Saray; *Limassol,* the Miramare and Curium Palace; *Famagusta,* and neighbouring *Varosha* (the *Golden Sands*), Grecian, Constantia, Florida, King George, Esperia Tower, Cypriana, Golden Mariana and Savoy; *Salamis,* Evagoras Court; *Larnaca,* Four Lanterns; *Paphos,* New Olympus; *Kyrenia,* Dome, Rock Ruby, Dolphin; at nearby *Karavas,* Mare Monte; and in the hill resorts of Troodos the Forest Park and Splendid Hotels at *Platres,* Berengaria Hotel at *Prodhromos* and the Troodos Hotel at *Troodos* itself.

It would be thinkable for a hotel-bound visitor to pass months in Cyprus without once savouring Cypriot food, for perhaps nowhere else are the separate arts of home and foreign cooking so consistently practised. The island's connexion with the west, and in particular with Britain, enables the unadventurous to dine every evening *à la française* in the best hotels of the cities, or on roast beef and Yorkshire pudding at the family hostelries. Such diners will never confront pickled warblers or sheepshead soup. But a compromise is certainly the best solution.

Cypriot cuisine benefits above all from the sheer range of meats and dairy products, of vegetables, fruits, herbs and spices, many of them unavailable in northern countries. The Cypriot dish resembles the staples of Greek, Turkish and Levantine gastronomy, but is richer than its cousins across the Aegean and Caramanian Seas. The best meats are lamb, often prepared (as *souvlakia* in Greek or *shish kebab* in Turkish) on a spit or as spiced sausage (*sheftalia*), and pork, which can end up as smoked ham pickled in wine (*hiromeri*) or as *lounza,* a smoked pork fillet spiced with wine. More exciting are the composite recipes such as *moussaka* (minced meat baked with eggplant, marrow and herbs), beloved by every visitor to Greece; *dolmadhes* (Turkish *kabak dolmasi*) which are stuffed vine leaves; *tavas* or *firkin kebabi* (pot pourri of spiced meat with onions); *cherkes tavughu* (chicken prepared in a sauce of walnut and lemon); the savoury *koupes* (rissole pasties filled with minced meat, parsley and onions and rolled in *bourgourri,* crushed corn seed); *kattimeria* (dumplings stuffed with meat or egg) and *zalatina* (jellied pork served with peppers and laurel). More exotic are *ambelopoulia* or *pulya* (tiny warblers pickled in vinegar and eaten whole); *patcha* (a stew of sheepshead garnished with lemon and garlic) and snails, particularly good from the Karpas. Fish is rare. As company to the main courses one cannot neglect *avgolemono* or "wedding soup" (a soup of rice, eggs and lemon), *taramosalata* (ground roes done in herbs), *hummus* (crushed chick-peas with olive oil, garlic and parsley) and a wealth of vegetables: huge tomatoes, eggplants, peppers, marrows and artichokes, also rice (in *pilav* dishes) and preparations of wheat, olives and sesame, all staples of the Cypriot regimen.

As for puddings there is no end to them; *lokmadhes* or *lokma* (hot doughnuts in syrup), *shamishi* (honey pancakes), *tiropites* and *eliopites* (cheese and olive pastries), *keshkül* (cornflour mould with almonds) and the sweet Near Eastern perennials of *halva, kadaif* and *baklava.* Fruits are prolific; all species thrive, from figs, apples and pomegranates to lemons-with-everything. Of cheeses, the salty white *haloumi* the milder *kefalotiri* (not unlike gruyère) and the creamy *kaskavali* are most favoured, though *feta* (from sheep or goat milk) is common enough in villages. A century ago Cypriot bread was considered second to none but that of the Sultan himself. Especially good today are *koulouri,* bread rolls studded with sesame seed and sold from many a street barrow. Bread, always essential to the peasant, is actually venerated in country cottages; no crumbs should ever be crushed under foot, no slices allowed to fall on the floor. Spilled olive oil is an evil omen, while the pouring of wine is, in simple households, considered an augury of fortune.

The origins of the vine go unrecorded but classical writers, Strabo and Pliny among them, alluded to the delicacy of Cypriot wines. The Crusaders patronised them in mediaeval Europe and they are mentioned in the chronicles of Richard Lionheart. The famous *Commandaria,* the dulcet dessert wine still bottled in Limassol and exported to all continents, has the oldest tradition of any named wine in the world. It owes its appellation to the *commanderies* or fiefs held by the Knights Templar during Frankish rule and it was such early connoisseurs who ensured its appearance at Plantagenet feasts in England. This fine liquor is nurtured on the chocolate soils of the metamorphous Troodos, but there are others of different flavour grown on the cretaceous limestone of neighbouring valleys, notably the ruby *St Hilarion* and the drier *Othello* and *White Lady,* or the honeyed white *Aphrodite,* to name but a few. Cyprus offers good sherry and a beer of its own, served cool and often going by the name of one of the Limassol breweries. Preceding the meal – or even replacing it, for such is its variety – is the habit of *mezedakia* or *"meze"*, appetisers of olive, salami, hummus, cheese and so forth, ready companions for wine or for *ouzo,* the heady spirit of anise which goes cloudy when water is added, and is the Greek equivalent of the Arabic *arak* and Turkish *raki*. The caller at a Cypriot house may as a courtesy be given *gliko* (fruits preserved in syrup); this is accepted, together with a glass of water.

Tourism, citrus, carobs, olives and wines: these, with copper, iron, chrome, manganese, asbestos and gypsum, excavated since earliest times, are the most important sources of the national income. Indeed the very word "Cyprus" denotes either a mineral or a vegetable – scholars still argue the point. Certainly the island's first industry, copper – known as *sunbar* to the Sumerians, was worked by Phoenicians close to the present mining centre of Xeros and the Romans were later to refer to this mineral as *aes cyprium* to distinguish it from bronze. At the same time it may have been the henna plant, known in Greek as *kypros,* which once prospered in Cyprian fields, that engendered the island's name.

The Cypriot calendar is replete with pagan festivals and religious holidays. Outstanding are the Orange Festivals celebrated in February and May, respectively, for the two harvests of Famagusta and Morphou; the Lemon Festival at Karavas; Mardi Gras at Limassol; Greek Easter Week with its Procession of the Epitaph; the Flower Festivals of Larnaca and Famagusta known as *Anthestiria* and held during May, formerly in honour of Aphrodite, now for Cypriot womankind in general; then at Whitsuntide all the coastal towns celebrate, on an epic and exuberant scale, the truly Cyprian *Cataclysmos* or Sea Games, best seen at Larnaca and Limassol. In June at lower Paphos the church still commemorates, with Byzantine splendour, the Feast of St Paul which marks the Pauline mission to Cyprus. The Archbishop, assisted by the entirety of his bishops, and a procession of icons, thread through the streets of Graeco-Roman Paphos. At Platres in late August the mountain people of Troodos gather to make music, and in the last week of September, Limassol stages a Wine Festival, its munificence running to free draughts for all. Christmas is signalled by the pine or cypress tree, and this is kept for fourteen days.

As to cultural activities, the amphitheatres of Salamis, Soli and Curium lend themselves to concerts, Greek tragedy and starlight Shakespeare. In other times "Othello" was shown at Othello's Tower in Famagusta. On summer days Kyrenia and Bellapais together play host to an International Festival of Music and Drama, while Nicosia enjoys a full season in winter. Finally an International Trade Fair brings the commercial world to Nicosia in September.

After an historical introduction (Chapter 2) the chapters that follow divide the island into regions. All of these save two (Morphou and Troodos) correspond roughly to the districts of the administrative map, and each tends to form a natural unit. The traveller who lands by air will necessarily start at *Nicosia* (Chapter 3) with its mediaeval city, its invaluable Cyprus Museum and many good hotels which can, incidentally, serve as a base for the whole island. A short motor ride takes one to *Kyrenia* (Chapter 4), the Portofino of the east enhanced by a stalwart fortress and by the beauties of its highland backdrop and rugged shoreline. Above the town loom the ethereal castles of Buffavento and St Hilarion, prototypes for Disneyland, and the ineffable abbey at Bellapais, set in luxuriant groves of olives and citrus. Adjacent to *Morphou* (Chapter 5) is a complete range of typical Cypriot landscapes and monuments, among them the classical relics at Vouni and Soli, a reddish coast dotted with villages now Greek now Turkish, and the brilliant frescoes of the Comnenian period at Asinou and Lagoudhera.

Across the Mesaoria are the beckoning contours of the *Troodos* (Chapter 6), the central massif of Cyprus renowned for the winter resorts perched on its Olympian shoulders, for monasteries crouched in its wooded shadows and for a rusticity and remoteness which, one hopes, will outlive the incursions of our century. In the far west, where Nicosia practically vanishes from mind – for such is the contrast – we come to *Paphos* (Chapter 7) which, in its various stages, appears often in Cypriot history, especially in classical times. Aphrodite (who is not only Roman Venus but the Phoenician Astarte) was born from the foam (*aphros*) of the Paphiot shore, but she was only the first in a line of eminences from that district. Today quiet churches and monasteries abound in the dappled valleys of the west and nowhere in Cyprus does so dreamy a view unfold as that from Fontana Amorosa.

On the southern shore lies *Limassol* (Chapter 8), Limassol of the vineyards, of Crusader Kolossi, of Richard Lionheart and Queen Berengaria. Sea and mountains conspire in the setting of nearby Curium and its forlorn neighbour the

Temple of Apollo. On the ruins of ancient Citium stands *Larnaca* (Chapter 9), for long a town which throve on the trades of seaborne Europeans, today oddly forgotten. Of all the Muslim buildings in Cyprus, the Tekke of Hala Sultan, rising on the far side of the Salt Lake from Larnaca, occupies the most imposing situation. A country road leads west from here, passing the mosaic church of Kiti and proceeding to the neolithic settlement at Khirokitia and the lace-making town of Lefkara, cradled in the mountains.

The eastern extremity of Cyprus has a personality fashioned by the sea and the breezy sweep of its low hills. *Famagusta and the Karpas Peninsula* (Chapter 10) are a microcosm of the island. Salamis has the pride of Graeco-Roman remains in Cyprus and Famagusta-within-the-Walls is a living museum of the Middle and Ottoman Ages. At Varosha the Golden Sands are graced with yachts, parasols and all the amenities of beach life. In contrast the Karpas, with miles of unvisited coastline and one of the most genial sceneries in the Mediterranean, thrusts ever further out to sea, which is to say it rather turns its back on the mainland. The book concludes (Chapter 11) with lists of Useful Information for the intending traveller.

CHAPTER TWO

Cyprus Past

*Who are the Cypriots? – The Island's prehistory – The
Island's mythology – Greek, Oriental and Western strains in
Cypriot history – Mycenae, Phoenicia, Anatolia, Macedonia,
Persia and Rome – Byzantium and Christianity – Richard
Lionheart and England's first connection with Cyprus –
Gothic efflorescence under Lusignans and Venetians – The
Turkish period – Early travellers – British rule and the
Republic*

Although one of the world's youngest states, the Republic of
Cyprus, independent since 1960, has a recorded history of
close on eight thousand years, during much of which time
the island was subject to a continuous occupation by foreign
powers. This fact and the island's Greek inheritance from the
Mycenaean era are the two salient points of Cypriot history.
Since the neolithic dawn when such places as Khirokitia were
settled, a central position has brought Cyprus in contact with
both the Aegean and Near Eastern worlds and made it a
stepping-stone for maritime peoples whose goal was the conquest not of Cyprus itself but rather of its mainland neigh-
bours. Cyprus has in consequence provided a conduit rather
than a source of civilisations. The prehistoric natives of
Cyprus, the Eteocypriots, were of Anatolian stock, Aryan like
the Hittites, but, till the advent of Achaeans in the second
millenium, of neither Greek blood nor Greek language.

The Achaeans came from Mycenae first as merchants and then as colonisers; though racially assimilated by the Eteo-cypriots (whose tongue survived at Amathus, near Limassol, into the 4th century B.C.), they soon established a cultural and commercial ascendency and laid the cornerstone of an Hellenic civilisation which, however affected by subsequent oriental and western European influences, continues vitally to this day. Whether we regard the history and arts of Cyprus as those of oriental Greeks or of hellenised orientals, their historic continuity is plain. The survival of certain bronze age arts, such as the manufacture of mud-bricks, or gourd carving, or the persistence of Homeric vocabulary in the island's Greek vernacular suggest that in many ways the island's cultural evolution has been less radical than that of Rhodes, Crete or mainland Greece.

In addition to the initial and enduring impact of the Greeks on Cyprus, whether Helladic, Hellenic, Hellenistic or Byzantine, two other determinants of the island's historic character have been, firstly, oriental (Anatolian, Phoenician, Assyrian, Egyptian, Persian, Arab, Turkish, Muslim) and secondly occidental (Roman, Crusader, Frankish, English, Genoese or Venetian and, most recently, British). The visitor to Cyprus today will be constantly reminded of this motley pageant as he travels between jet airport and Gothic churches converted to Turkish mosques, as he leaps centuries from Mycenaean Enkomi to Roman Salamis, from the Phoenician Idalium (modern Dhali) to the Venetian campanile of many a village, or simply from room to room of the Cyprus Museum.

The semi-mythology of early Cyprus is related in Homeric literature. Paphos had a legendary founder in King Cinyras who sent a breastplate to Agamemnon for his Trojan campaign, and popularised the cult of Aphrodite, soon revered in other Cyprian cities like Tamassus and Amathus. In Greek myth Aphrodite's birth-place was always envisaged at Petra tou Romiou, an evocative chalk monolith piercing the coral waters of south-western Cyprus. But Aphrodite was a hellenisation of Astarte, Ishtor and Ashtaroth, native to ancient Syria and Palestine. Likewise Adonis, the reputed son of Cinyras, was also the Phoenician Tammuz (*adon* being the Phoenician word for "lord"). But if Tammuz was killed whilst hunting in the Lebanese hills, Adonis died at Idalium in central Cyprus. In the course of centuries Aphrodite and Adonis were paired in the popular mind. For the pleasure of Pygmalion, both amateur sculptor and Cyprian King, Aphrodite animated the voluptuous statue of Galatea, celebrated by Ovid and W. S. Gilbert and much elaborated, as Eliza Doolittle, by G. B. Shaw. Aphrodite presided over many a love match, bringing fame to old Paphos where her cult was centred, and in later time "Cyprian" became synonymous with "lascivious". A fifteenth century Pope described the wantonness of ancient Cyprus as follows: "before giving their virgins in marriage the Cypriots were accustomed to offer them to strangers and to sailors seeking their shores. Not without reason did antiquity declare Cyprus to Venus."

After the Trojan War (*c.* 1250 B.C.) and the collapse of Mycenae (1200–1100), a fresh wave of Achaean migrants appears to have reached the island and it was then, according to tradition, that Teucer, son of Telamon, founded Salamis, naming it after the Attic isle which was one day to witness the defeat of Xerxes' navy. In this Helladic or late bronze age, Mycenaean arts and Minoan writing contributed powerfully to the civilisation of Cyprus. Archaeology has unearthed more Mycenaean pottery in Cyprus than in Argos itself; whether this originated on the island is debatable, but Cypriot vases of the time do indicate a predilection for particular genres such as amphoras decorated with chariot scenes. Helladic Cyprus, moreover, betrays a general indifference to the *tholos* tombs and the small bronze votive figures so typical of Argolid Mycenae. Greeks in Cyprus thus recreated an Hellenic world *sui generis*, and during successive centuries of political isolation from Greece, wove a composite fabric from ancestral memories of Mycenae and Crete on one hand and from organic links with Hittites, Assyrians, Egyptians and other cultures of the Near East on the other. Escaping, unlike Rhodes and Mycenae itself, the Dorian invasions of the late Bronze Age, the Cypriots did preserve intact a civilisation that included kingship and the knowledge of writing.

Since it lies in the shadow of the Asian continent, Cyprus was inexorably to fall under the sway of Phoenicia. Astarte, metallurgical skills and ceramic styles were among the more remarkable importations. There were Phoenician settlements at Citium, Amathus and elsewhere; their collaboration during the Ionian Revolt of the Anatolian Greeks enabled the Persians to impose their rule on Cyprus for two centuries (550–322 B.C.). The Periclean and Aristotelean ages of Athens thus touched upon Cyprus only indirectly but the Greek idea survived. Evagoras I of Salamis, whom the Athenian Isocrates regarded as a model ruler, attempted a short-lived political revival of Hellenism in 374 B.C. His work was consummated when, in 333 B.C., Cyprus declared for Alexander the Great and contributed one hundred and twenty ships to the fleet of Macedon. After Alexander's death (323 B.C.), Cyprus passed under the Ptolemaic aegis and was divided into four districts, Paphos, Amathus, Lapithos and Salamis, each administered by a *strategos* or military appointee of the court at Alexandria. A feature of this period was the establishment of the *koinon* or union of cities which evolved under the Roman emperors as a religious institution, known as the *Koinon Kyprion*.

The cultural and especially commercial vigour of the island was promoted by the Romans (58 B.C.–A.D. 395) who worked the copper mines and issued silver coins depicting the Temple of Aphrodite at Paphos. Cicero came from Rome as third governor. The Temple was rebuilt by Augustus after an earthquake, and Palaia Paphos (Old Paphos) continued as capital. Salamis flourished too, for a forum, aqueduct, gymnasium and, of course, baths were erected there.

The outstanding event of the Roman epoch was the intro-duction, in A.D. 45, of Christianity by Paul and Barnabas, the latter a native Cypriot, who preached the new religion to Hebrew settlers. The slow process of conversion was com-pleted by the 5th century, thanks to the zeal of a succession of great Cypriot clerics and saints: Heraclides, Lazarus, Spy-ridon, Philon and Epiphanios among them. The Jewish popu-lation of Cyprus, which was substantial, proved as inimical to Christianity as the pagan Greeks, and during the reign of Trajan the new religion was practically annihilated.

In the same years Rome itself subscribed to Christ. The new religion was formally adopted in A.D. 313 and in 330 Constantine the Great removed the imperial seat to the ancient *polis* of the Bosphorus, Byzantium, renaming it Con-stantinople. By the late 4th century the Church of Cyprus was fully established and the old pagan temples were replaced by basilican churches. Apollo and Orpheus gave way to Christ, Aphrodite to the Virgin. The timely discovery (in 488) by Anthemius, Archbishop of Cyprus, of the relics of St Barnabas near Salamis (named Constantia following the earthquakes of 334 and 345) reminded the Emperor Zeno of the apostolic origins of the Cypriot Church. The Emperor forthwith granted it not only an autocephalous status; he also conferred upon its Archbishop the imperial privileges of wearing a purple cloak, carrying a sceptre in lieu of the customary staff and signing documents in red ink. The Church's autonomy, along with its symbols, have survived to our own day, and they bestow a prestige and political authority unparalleled in Orthodox countries except, perhaps, at Mount Athos. Indeed since the 4th century, when the island's ecclesiastics assumed the mantle of the pre-Christian *Koinon Kyprion,* the Church has acted as the prime guarantor of Greek cultural and poli-tical unity. Thus Frankish and Venetian endeavours in the Middle Ages to Latinise the islanders by suppressing Ortho-doxy had quite the opposite effect of strengthening the Hellenism of Cypriot Christians, and throughout the Turkish period the peculiar predominance of the Orthodox clergy in Cyprus effectively ensured the survival of the Greek community.

As the crescent of Islam accompanied the Arab conquests of the Christian Near East, so did the star of independent Byzantium flicker ever more precariously until, unsustained by the Latins, it was finally snuffed out by the Turks in 1453. Between the 7th and 10th centuries Cyprus was subject to continuous raiding and occasional occupation by the Arabs. For defensive reasons the capital was moved to Ledra (Nicosia) at the island's centre. The half-fictional Akritas Dighenis performed acts of superhuman heroism in Cypriot resistance to Saracen inroads, but in some respects the Arab presence was less onerous than the Byzantine, as Moorish rule in Spain often proved more beneficent than that of the Christian Frank. But few Christian edifices survived in Cyprus unharmed; the superb mosaics remaining nowadays at Kiti and Kanakaria churches (near Larnaca and in the Karpas respectively) hint at the sophistication which had marked the Christian arts before the Arab incursions. Nevertheless the Church itself was preserved and in the 11th, 12th and 13th centuries generated a spate of building. Churches like Asinou and Lagoudhera, such monasteries as Kykko in the northern Troodos (where an icon supposedly painted by St Luke is retained), Makheras (in the eastern Troodos) and Ayios Neophytos near Paphos, all are living representatives of a kind of golden age in Cypriot Orthodoxy.

In 1184 one Isaac Comnenus proclaimed himself Despot of Cyprus and soon evinced an ineptitude and recklessness which combined to bring his downfall. From St Neophytus we learn (1196) that Isaac "not only utterly despoiled the land, but every day hounded and oppressed its nobles." From the same decade dates the first English connexion with the island. At a time when Richard Lionheart had joined Philip II of France and the Holy Roman Emperor on the Third Crusade, Richard's bride-elect, Berengaria of

Navarre was storm-blown upon Cyprus as she journeyed from Sicily to the embattled city of Acre. Isaac refused her refuge, as a contemporary chronicler, Benedict, Abbot of Peterborough, describes:

> Isaac seized the chattels of those who were drowned and robbed of their money all who escaped from the shipwreck. Moreover in the fury of his savagery, worse than any beast of prey, he refused permission to enter the port to a galliot which had been driven there by the wind and which carried the Queen of Sicily.

Richard hastened to her aid. Once he had married his Berengaria at Limassol, he brought Isaac to heel at Famagusta, where the tyrant was despatched, in silver chains, to the Syrian castle of Margat. As it happened Isaac was the island's last Greek-speaking ruler till 1960.

Richard's reign proved to be an interregnum. Being hard pressed for funds, he sold the island to the Knights Templar who in turn, suffering shortages of manpower, had their valuable but vulnerable outpost transferred to Guy de Lusignan, who was the titular King of Jerusalem and a vassal of the Holy Roman Emperor. During the three ensuing centuries of Lusignan domination, Cyprus enjoyed an independence from external control, and the Frankish dynasty presided over an efflorescence of the arts, of pomp and wealth. Lusignan Cyprus possessed a model constitution: its laws were a pattern of mediaeval jurisprudence; the riches of Famagusta vied with those of Venice, and the soaring cathedrals of Famagusta and Nicosia, the splendid abbey at Bellapais and the commanding fortresses of St Hilarion, Buffavento and Kantara, all products of a Gothic genius, helped in the Frankish mind to compensate for the Crusaders' loss of the Holy Land. But the institution of serfdom was a yoke upon the Greek peasantry and the tyranny of the Latin Church an insult and challenge to Byzantine tradition. In consequence the brilliant culture of the Lusignans, and of the Venetians

Frescoes at Asinou Church

Salamis

who followed, was only superficially reflected in the quality of indigenous Cyprus. True the Cypriot writer Leontios Makheras introduced in the 13th century the sonnet form into Greek literature. Certainly the townsmen of Famagusta were bejewelled in the western style; undoubtedly the Bedestan in Nicosia shows a fusion of east and west, as the pointed arch was universally adopted by Cypriot architects and as a number of icons betray a Venetian inspiration. But the rural heart of Cyprus rested loyal to the spirit of Byzantium. Its Greek language kept its Homeric idiom; its monasteries mirrored, in icon-painting, the rather rigid Paleologue style of the 14th and 15th centuries.

Cyprus passed to Venice when Catherine Cornaro, the Venetian wife of the last Lusignan king, James II, and a descendant of the Roman Cornelii, allowed the Republic to force her abdication in 1489. This romantic figure now retired to the miniature court of Asolo, pictured amusingly in the *Asolani* of Cardinal Bembo. The Venetians ruled Cyprus as a province for the same time-span as the later British (eighty-two years), and their interest in the fortifications of Nicosia, Kyrenia and Famagusta notably exceeded their concern for the islanders. Orthodoxy was persecuted and the populace further pressed beneath the feudal weight. Compared with Crete, where the Venetians governed from 1210 to 1669, their legacy to Cyprus was a spare one, limited to military construction, some aspects of church building and a few loans to rustic parlance such as *pomilori* ("tomatoes") and *viva* (for the Greek *yasu,* pronounced when raising one's glass).

Although the Ottoman conquest of Cyprus, effected between 1570 and 1572 under the command of Lala Mustafa Pasha, was fraught with daily horror, the Greeks of Cyprus—as is usual in a transfer of foreign power—welcomed the Turks as saviours, from feudalism and religious intolerance. Thus too were the British acclaimed, three centuries later. The Turks coveted Cyprus for itself and for the defences which it afforded at the moment of their naval supremacy in the eastern Mediterranean :

OTHELLO : What is the matter, think you?
CASSIO : Something from Cyprus, as I may divine :
    It is a business of some heat.
FIRST SENATOR :
    When we consider the
    Importancy of Cyprus to the Turk.

The Hispano-Hapsburg defeat of the Ottomans at Lepanto (1571) freed most of Western Europe from the menace of a Muslim imperialism but established a Turco-Spanish balance farther east. For three centuries the eastern Mediterranean was to remain under Turkish domination. Cyprus suffered the immediate ravages of invasion. Nicosia and Famagusta became melancholy shades of their resplendent past and Limassol and Paphos shrunk to the proportions of a village. But the feudal order was abolished, and Orthodoxy, always preferred by the Turks to the Latin Church, fully re-instated, in its traditionally autocephalous form. While Latin churches such as the Cathedral of St Nicholas, Famagusta and St Sophia at Nicosia were converted to Muslim use, the Greek clerics of Cyprus, whose freedom of action compared well even with that of the favoured Greek hierarchs in Constantinople and the Greek-speaking phanariots who formed the Ottoman bureaucracy, enjoyed at times an almost absolute power over the island's Muslims, a factor leading to tragic results in 1821. "Cinderella of the Mediterranean", as Cyprus was termed by an English traveller, could at least choose her own rags.

Of the Ottoman forces which had effected the conquest, some twenty thousand remained in Cyprus, not merely as a garrison but as settlers in an island severely depopulated. These were Muslims from Anatolia, many of whom doubtless possessed similar pre-Seljuk and pre-Ottoman origins as the Greeks of Cyprus, Ionia and Pontus – though few Greeks or

Turks, in an age of ethnocentrisms, will ever admit as much. In a world where racial purity is non-existent (especially so in lands such as the Balkans, Greece, and Asia Minor which have been open to migration and foreign conquest) it is evident that the modern Turk is both the child of an Asiatic horde and of a settled Anatolian stock. Thus the Ottoman coloniser of Cyprus had in his veins the blood of Phrygian, Lydian, and Cappadocian ancestors as well as that of his obvious Turkic (and Kurdish and Armenian) forebears. He may himself have been a recent convert from Greek or Nestorian Christianity. The Greeks themselves are composite too. Nikos Kazantzakis is rightly proud of this distinction : "Just as the peoples of ancient Greece were a mixture of the most varied races, young and old, European and Oriental, so our own contemporary people, with its great and unrelenting strength, has absorbed Slavs, Albanians, Franks, Arabs and Turks. A new blend."* And in a meticulous study an English scholar has described the oriental character of Byzantium as it evolved *before* the Fall of Constantinople.† The Graeco-Turkish contest of five centuries, like the intercommunal feud of the Irish, has its roots not in an absolute division between two races, but in the rivalry of religions, a tension between victor and vanquished, a nostalgia for former frontiers and a reluctance to forget the excesses of the past.

Once they arrived in Cyprus, however, the Turks were segregated. There were soldiers manning a permanent garrison, at first 1000 janissaries and 2666 saphis, a strength which had dwindled to token figures by the 1860's. With their hopes of intervention by the Christian powers (above all Savoy and Tuscany) doomed to unfulfilment, the Cypriot Greeks could merely acquiesce in the deepening stagnation of Cypriot economic life and console themselves in the legitimate conduct of church and local affairs. They were empowered to appoint

---

* *Travels in Greece,* Oxford, 1966, p. 166.
† Sir William Ramsay, "The intermixture of races in Asia Minor" in *Proceedings of the British Academy,* London, 1915–16.

a *dragoman* (literally "interpreter") from the Christian population. With his right of direct access to the Sultan, he won frequent concessions for his people—and the envy of many Turks. Conditions might have been worse. Unlike Sardinia, Corsica and Crete, Cyprus was spared the scourge of brigandage and the ferocity of the vendetta. The curses of plague, locusts and earthquake were not, after all, man-made. Each electing its own headman or *muktar,* the Greek and Turkish communities more often than not coexisted, and co-operated. Apathy or resignation was more characteristic a defect than animosity. Not until 1788 was the Turkish occupation of Cyprus first chronicled by a Greek – the Archimandrite Kyprianos.

The Greek appetite for national liberation was whetted in Cyprus only when it had consumed the forebearance of the Morean Greeks, on the eve of the Greek War of Independence. As for the Turkish minority, it had little marginal advantage over the Greeks in an island which it came to regard as home. For Turkish Cypriots Istanbul seemed as distant as was Constantinople for the Greeks.

The isolation of Cyprus was not absolute. A long train of northern visitors, envoys, merchants, pilgrims bound for Jerusalem, peripatetic people, eccentrics, passed through the island. In the 18th and early 19th centuries they included an English-born Muslim who posed successfully as a Turk and Persian by turns, a Spanish diarist who feigned the title and personality of one Ali Bey el Abassi – self-proclaimed "son of Othman Bey of Aleppo and descendant of Abbas, uncle of Mohamed", Frederik Hasselqvist, an emissary of the Swedish king who had his Cypriot diaries edited by Linnaeus, and Vassily Varsky, a Russian priest – chronicler from Kiev whose tireless peregrinations between monasteries produced the best commentary on Cypriot monastic life in our possession. Over the same years foreign consuls were accredited to Larnaca, which now rode the steep wave of its commerce. English entrepreneurs installed mansions in the foothills of the Troodos and their tomb-stones still stand in the churchyard of St Lazarus at Larnaca.

The Greek clergy, as we have seen, exercised in 18th century Cyprus an authority unmatched in the Ottoman Empire. From his palace in Nicosia the Ethnarch administered the whole island, appointed the local officials and was responsible for assessing and collecting taxes levied annually and sent to the Imperial Treasury. All the islanders, Turkish and Greek alike, looked upon him rather than the *Muhassil* as *de facto* Governor. The supreme power of the Archbishops attained its apogee in the reigns of Selim III and Mustafa IV, and was unshaken until, in 1804, the financially oppressed Turkish population in vain rose up against the ecclesiastic power.

The Greeks reacted as a community. In 1812 Archbishop Kyprianos founded a school which later became the Pancyprian Gymnasium, enshrining the ideals of Byzantine and classical Greece. Gradually the unrest preceding the Greek Revolution, in Morea, Attica, Thessaly and the Isles, affected Cypriot Greeks as well. Archbishop Kyprianos was inducted into the revolutionary Philike Hetairia and in 1821, when the first shots of the War in Greece were fired at Patras, the Grand Vizir, Kuchuk Mehmet, decided on pre-emptive measures against further Greek aggrandisement in Cyprus. He disarmed all Greeks, not only of their weapons, but of household tools and butchers' knives. Certain Cypriots were accused of secret correspondence with the insurrectionaries of Hydra. On 9th July, 1821, Archbishop Kyprianos was hanged from a mulberry tree, outside the Saray; the Bishops of Paphos, Citium and Kyrenia were beheaded and their corpses tossed into the square. This was the signal for a massacre of the Greek leadership in general and of the clergy in particular. A resident Frenchman, the Comte de Mas Latrie, relates how, before killing them, the executioners saddled the priests of Phaneromeni Monastery as they would their horses, breaking their teeth to force the bits into their

35

mouths and having them caper under their spurs. While the peasantry escaped to the hills, more fortunate Greeks sought refuge with the European consuls. Some two hundred perished.

Thus while the year 1821 spelled the dawn of Greek independence on parts of the mainland, a more rigorous Ottoman overlordship was imposed on the Cypriots. In order to stem the tide of national resistance among the disaffected nationalities of his Empire and to achieve reforms at home, the Sultan in 1839 embarked on a programme of westernisation, the *Tanzimat*. But as wars of liberation continued to flare in the Balkans and Egypt, the Great Powers were sucked into a vortex of rival solutions to the Eastern Question. Russia's embroilment in the affairs of Turkey, dramatised by the Crimean episode, became a constant feature of Near Eastern geopolitics; thus when in 1878 the Tsar's army stood before the gates of Constantinople, Great Britain, finding herself the only thalassocracy capable of countering Russian moves in the area, concluded at Berlin a formal treaty whereby she guaranteed against tsarist designs the integrity of the Sultan's realm, in return for the promise of Turkish internal reform—and the cession of Cyprus to British administration, even if the Sultan was to retain nominal suzerainty.

The transference of the island to Britain was greeted with enthusiasm by Greeks and Turks alike. For the former she was not only a Christian democracy but also a nation (or so they believed) of Byronic Philhellenes which fifteen years back had freely ceded the Ionian Isles to Greece. For the latter she represented a bulwark against Russia by the terms of Berlin. The young Kitchener, of later imperial fame, sent by the Foreign Office to make a land survey of the island, remarked on New Year's Eve, 1878, that "while the clocks were chiming the advent of another year, shouts and cheers for Victoria and the English woke us up." Queen Victoria, it was supposed, would favour *enosis,* or union with Greece. Cypriot hopes were not fully justified.

As it happened the "other island" was not unknown to Cypriots. After Richard Lionheart's brief sojourn, there were further exchanges. In 1362 a tournament held at Smithfield had featured Cypriot knights. The Lusignan King Peter I visited England and from the 17th century onwards the Levant Company, employing "tall ships belonging to London, Southampton and Bristol", did regular trade with Larnaca. In the eyes of a Dutch envoy (c. 1700): "The English consul's home is the best on the whole island . . . he is respected, as he advances money to the inhabitants, for getting in their several harvests. Interest rate (twenty per cent) is received in silk, wine, cotton and other local products."

In 1878 the commercial value of a Cypriot acquisition was not lost on the British. Observers spoke of "aromatic tobacco of the most delicate quality . . . the wine Homer praised," of gold and copper, "caves of jaspar and agate." But other justifications were advanced as well. High-minded ones: "Our moral influence among all the nations of the East, our protection of Mahometan Turkey cannot fail to endear us to the Mussulman population of Hindostan." Cyprus would itself be regenerated, for the good of its populace. There were political reasons: a preponderant authority would be borne over the councils of the Sublime Porte. And finally strategic ones: "Cyprus holds the key of the Egyptian valley through which a railway to expedite our passage to India will be laid down sooner or later."

Cyprus meant all things to all men visiting it shortly after the British occupation of 1878. The *Spectator* referred to the island as a "splendid garden, a sanatorium for the invalids of Europe." Naval officers stationed in Syria regarded it as a haven of health. Some were fascinated by the womenfolk, "handsomer than in the other Greek isles," while for Sir Samuel Baker, who was far from being a Cypriophobe, a "close inspection of all women and girls showed that their throats and breasts were literally covered with ancient and modern fleabites." The same traveller found Cypriot mule-

tracks a little hazardous for his peculiar means of transport –
a gypsy caravan shipped from England for the purpose. In
the towns, he notes, the height of this eccentric vehicle inter-
fered with the roofs and water-spouts of the one-storey houses.
Some visitors recorded their cordial detestation of the beggars
and the absence of plumbing. Others extolled the abundance
of hares, francolins and partridge. At the outset of his career
Kitchener foresaw the kind of evolution which the British
Government should supervise:

> There are many places in the island waiting for the hand
> of the capitalist to change them from barren wastes to
> their former fruitfulness. All that is required is enterprise
> and capital.

Kitchener's exotic manners endeared the young subaltern to
the islanders. In Nicosia he kept a bear-cub as a pet and cultivated, for the first time, the famous walrus moustache.

Undoubtedly Whitehall's handling of Cypriot administration, economic life, communications, education and health was
as a rule well-intentioned and frequently successful. Forests
grew again in the Troodos. The scourges of malaria and
locusts were removed; literacy spread in two generations – so
that today ninety per cent of the population can read, and
living standards rose by the 1930s to outpace those of all
other lands of the eastern Mediterranean. Britain, however,
was required to remit to the Turkish Treasury a heavy tribute,
equalling all profits from the island's revenue, until 1914,
when Cyprus was, in the war interest, annexed to the British
crown. That the new responsibilities to the Cypriots were to
be imperfectly discharged reflected less on the island's Governors, who were often, like Sir Ronald Storrs and Sir Harry
Luke, sensitive and scholarly Philhellenes, than on the ten-
dency of the Colonial Office to undervalue the island's
economy and underestimate the force of national feeling
among the Greeks.

True, in 1915 the Asquith Government promised the

Cypriots *enosis,* on condition that Greece, whose support was urgently solicited in Serbia, join the War on the Allied side. A pro-German orientation caused the Government in Athens (which was yet to include Venizelos) to refuse, and the *enosis* offer lapsed. Cypriots fought alongside Britain in two World Wars. But the divisive issues of *enosis* and the proportionate representation of the Greek and Turkish communities in local government continued to simmer in the inter-war years till in 1931 an uprising of Greek Cypriots prompted the British to deport the two bishops espousing most vocally the unionist cause.

Twenty-five years afterwards Archbishop Makarios III, today President of the Republic, was exiled in like fashion (to the Seychelles) while between 1955 and 1959 a guerrilla war of national liberation, led by General (then Colonel) Grivas and his National Organisation of Cypriot Fighters (*Ethniki Organosis Kyprion Agoniston,* EOKA), raged in the towns and hills, and a tripartite diplomatic contest involving London, Athens and Ankara further eroded goodwill between the two communities. The twin slogans of *enosis* and *taxim* (partition) became the poles to which Greek and Turk, respectively, gravitated.

The Troubles, or the Emergency, as the optimists prefer to call the Cypriot Revolution, came at a conjunction of three historic forces, affecting more than Cyprus alone. Greek nationalism (or the *megali idea*), Turkish republican nationalism and Britain's withdrawal from Empire combined to pose what Arnold Toynbee has termed the Western Question in the Græco-Turkish sphere. That question is not yet fully resolved, but the independence of Cyprus declared in 1960 on the unsteady rock of agreements made in Zurich and London at least removed the frustration of alien rule and, paradoxically, reconciled the island to its former rulers. By gaining statehood Cyprus has probably passed a watershed, and the uneasy peace between its two main communities (the Greeks are 79 per cent and the Turks 18 per cent), too readily

39

disturbed in the early 1960s, now appears less ambiguous, more hopeful.

The foreign visitor may be shocked to find in Nicosia and Famagusta divided cities reminiscent of Berlin and Londonderry, and on certain roads (notably at Kokkina on the northwest coast and between Kythrea and Lefkoniko) barricades at which blue-bereted UN patrols, as well as Greek and Turkish militia, are positioned in kiosks coloured with the appropriate symbols. The present book will not attempt to delude the reader into thinking that Graeco-Turkish differences are either entirely composed or else of no consequence. The differences both exist and matter. Nonetheless the foreigner, and more especially the tourist, will be scarcely if at all inconvenienced by the barrier already mentioned and he will feel at all times sincerely welcome among both communities – for whom hospitality is an unwritten tenet. Without perhaps knowing as much, he is building bridges.

CHAPTER THREE

Nicosia

*Topography and history – The mediaeval city within the
walls and its monuments – Turkish, Greek and Western
landmarks – The Cyprus Museum and Turkish Museum –
Modern Nicosia – Domestic living and marriage customs.*

Push open the shutters of the hotel window and a rectangle
of morning light brings a kinetic panorama. Across the ramparts of the old city, which is raised on a slight plateau, stand
six minarets, and from the tallest a muezzin proclaims the only
true faith. On the Greek side, beneath walls daubed with the
mottoes of *enosis* and anti-communism, a couple of soldiers
play chess in an overgrown garden.

Like the capitals of all new states Nicosia enjoys and
endures an exploding growth, outwards and upwards. Unlike
many new capitals it possesses a lustrous if checkered history.
Known till the 12th century of our era as Ledra, the city of
Nicosia (*Lefcosia* to the Greeks, *Lefkoçe* to the Turks) profited
from the fact of geographic centrality when the Saracen raids
jeopardised the coast. Dante alluded to its blandishments and
by the 15th century it boasted two hundred and fifty churches.
Today's city consists of mediaeval and modern parts, the
former ringed by a circular Venetian wall (a cartographer's
delight), the latter spilling out over the commodious plain.

Within its three miles of wall, the old city is itself divided,
on a rough ethnic pattern, the Greeks remaining in the

41

southern sector, and the Turks – against whom the Venetians intended their ramparts – relegated to the northern. Their physical partition unhappily takes the form of human detritus – heaped sacking, petrol cans and rusting cars. Foreigners find no difficulty in passing the check-points. Turkish commerce is still chiefly confined to the old town but the Greeks have opted for the spaces of Nicosia outside the walls and it is on a south-westerly course that their business, government, culture, pleasure and residence are set. The wide tree-lined avenues of modern Nicosia, fringed by villas and, most recently, by high-rise blocks of glass and concrete, by banks, boutiques, bars and airline offices, voice a theme of the modern Mediterranean, common to most cities from Tunis to Salonika.

Monuments are therefore, with a few exceptions such as the Cyprus Museum, situated inside the walls. In seeking them out a good map is needed, for the streets, ravines of tall houses lurching towards one another at tangents, run in an unpredictable maze. It is also well to remember that since buildings may be shut at odd times of the day, a custodian should first be found. In the case of Orthodox churches a key (*glidhi*) and often guidance are dispensed by the priest who, as in the Cypriot countryside, lives nearby. For the Muslim monuments in Nicosia the Turkish Tourist Office is the appropriate reference.

Mediaeval Nicosia is the work neither of Greek nor of Turk. Its walls, best seen from Stasinos Avenue, are guarded by eleven bastions named for prominent Italian families – such as Quirini and Roccas – and are the product of Venetian engineering. The city's finest showplace, Selimiye Mosque, once the Church of St Sophia, is a close cousin of the cathedrals at Rheims and Chartres. A late 14th century Italian voyager described it as "a fair and great church, vaulted, and the whole of the vault from the choir-arch to the high altar is painted with fine blue and golden stars." Founded in 1208 by Queen Alice of Champagne, wife of Henry I, the church took two centuries to build and served as the chapel royal of the Franks. The Lusignans were crowned here as Kings of Cyprus and many a chevalier was laid to rest under its slabs of honeyed stone. It performed its Latin purpose till 1570 when the Ottomans converted it into their principal mosque on the island. Muslim practice forbids human representation, with the result that at St Sophia all Christian paintings were whitewashed, the windows stripped of glass and most sculptures disfigured (two angels made a miraculous escape and still grace the western façade). Islam likewise demanded minarets for its muezzin and in 1571 two were made to sprout above the west towers of the Gothic church. From frontal view their slim and lofty silhouette appears lame and incongruous in relation to the rest – two "gigantic candles capped by extinguishers, as though altar tapers had been taken as their model," in the phrase of one detractor. But from north or south they are strangely consistent with the high arches of the nave. Although the church's basic architecture remains unscathed – and some may find the white and denuded spaces of the nave more satisfactory than the grey clutter of a church in Christian use – Muslim arts are much less happily superimposed on a Latin church than on, let us say, the great St Sophia of Constantinople, whose style engendered the best of Ottoman mosques such as the Sultan Ahmet (or Blue) Mosque in modern Istanbul. The "nave" of Selimiye Mosque is now hung with clusters of red and white electric bulbs; a green grandfather clock with Arabic facings keeps Mecca time; Koranic inscriptions girdle the walls. From a minaret the imam's prayerful wail charges the evening air. The entire building, its history and functions have somehow only an oblique relevance to Cyprus. And it never served the Greeks.

More versatile was the old Church of St Nicholas which, despite its 14th century Latin and Gothic origin served as the Orthodox *mitropolia* (cathedral) during the Venetian era and was later used by the Turks as a covered market. Hence the Turkish (or Persian) name by which it is called today, the Bedestan.

Walking from the Selimiye Mosque in westerly and northerly directions, one passes the main Turkish buildings of Nicosia. Some of these seem quite unaccustomed to admitting foreigners so that a pioneering spirit is of advantage. There is the Büyük Han (Great Inn) in Arasta Street, erected soon after the Turkish conquest to house foreign envoys and visiting merchants. In the middle is a fountain covered by a graceful octagonal *mesjid,* or chapel, approached from the outside by a spiral stairway. Like the *khaneh* of Arabs and Persians, this Han offered the traveller rest and victuals, and accommodation below for his animals. Its present occupants are plainly more sedentary and rather less affluent. Further west, at the top end of Victoria Street, rises the agreeable shape of a 16th century mosque originally conceived, it is said, on the instructions got in a dream by one Arab Ahmet Pasha, whose name it today bears. Its design follows the conventions of provincial Ottoman architecture: a simple octagon with red, white and green predominating inside, and a slender minaret sharpening to a pencil-point and surmounted by the Turkish crescent. Since religious Turks adhere strictly to the sterner precepts of Sunni Islam no images ornament the walls, only Koranic citations done in florid calligraphy. In the courtyard is the tomb of Kamil Pasha, a Grand Vizir of Cypriot provenance.

To the east of Selimiye Mosque is the Sultan's Library, named after the bibliophile Sultan Mahmud II who founded it in 1829. Though small it contains several illuminated Korans and texts in Turkish, Persian and Arabic script. Across the street, somewhat forlorn, is the Lapidarian Museum, housed in a restored 15th century structure and preserving several mediaeval sarcophagi, funerary tablets and inscriptions. Much of this quarter is sunk in desuetude; large tracts cry out for the builder's drill and mortar, and amidst a rubbly clearing stands the abandoned Yeni Jami (New Mosque), now no more than a lonely minaret in a children's playground.

Turkish business revolves about Atatürk Square, of which landmarks are the Saray Hotel and the Venetian Column, once crowned by the Venetians with a Lion of St Mark, now carrying a marble ball. From here Kyrenia Avenue, crammed with Armenian as well as Turkish enterprises, funnels traffic out through the Kyrenia Gate. Just before the Gate is the newly instituted Turkish Museum, housed in the former Tekke (Monastery) of the Mevlevi Dervishes, whose activities were proscribed in 1925 by the reforming Atatürk. The Mevlevi seat had as its spiritual father Jalal-ad-din Rumi, the most illustrious of all Persian Mystics. His poetry, particularly the Mathnavi, expounded those 14th century Sufi ideals of love, conciliation and cosmic unity which brought Islam closer to Christian and other religious belief:

The lamps are different, but the light
　is the same : it comes from Beyond.
O Thou who art the kernel of
　existence, the discord between
　Mohamedan, Zoroastrian and Jew
　is but a thing of private prejudice.

Rumi was born in the Afghan city of Balkh, in a country where Hellenistic influences (through Alexander the Great) no less than Buddhist ones preordained philosophical speculation and toleration. The Mevlevis always possessed a propensity for transcendentalism, and their liberal conduct facilitated the islamisation of the Anatolian Christians. In Turkey the Mevlevi Dervishes were celebrated for the whirling dances which they performed with a controlled passion. A *New York Times* article has described how these dances are revived once a year in the city of Konya (Iconium, later the Seljuk capital) where Rumi died in 1273. Some sixteen dervishes ("monks"), clad in gowns and tall fezzes, start their performance seated on the floor and with heads bowed in contemplation. A solitary voice intones by way of prelude and then, as the orchestra plays a plaintive melody in a minor key, the dancers begin to rotate, each performer gyrating with his right hand upturned in order that he may receive holy grace, while the downturned hand transmits it to earth. The dancers pivot counter-clock-wise on their left legs for stretches of up to two hours, but the dance ends abruptly as they drop to the floor, silent and expressionless.

The Mevlevi Tekke was the only one of its kind in Cyprus and was administered by sheikhs sent first from Turkey and latterly from Syria—until the last sheikh died in 1954. Their spirit still haunts the dancing-floor in the middle of their museum and it is not hard to envision the flautists and drum-mers seated in the gallery. Mevlevi costumes and instruments are exhibited here, together with Turkish Cypriot costumes, Ottoman coins and medals, prayer-rugs, the Koran of Lala Mustafa and a number of *fermans* (imperial decrees) and letter patents, each illuminated with the peacock shape of the imperial seal, as elegant in 1900 as in the day of Suleyman the Magnificent. A sepia photograph of the Grand Vizir, Kamil Pasha, posed in Cairo with King George V and Queen Mary, records the passing of an era. Next to the Tekke is a mausoleum containing the remains of sixteen sheikhs – and one wife – reposing austerely in tombs painted green like the tomb of Mohamed, and with headstones carved in the form of a Mevlevi hat. The courtyard, however, is more joyful; its tall cylindrical tombstones bear epitaphs for the men and floral engravings for the female dead.

Of Greek religious buildings in Nicosia there are many exemplars but few masterpieces, especially if we compare them with the churches and monasteries of the outlying countryside. Orthodoxy was at too obvious a disadvantage in the citadel of the Latins and Ottomans. Small wonder that, from the Arab invasions to the Troubles of the 1950s, Greek Orthodoxy preferred the safety of the hills. The Church of St John is an exception. This is situated next to the new Arch-bishop's Palace, which it serves. Its 18th century wall paint-ings are extremely late by Cypriot standards but their observance of the colours and stylistic conventions of Byzantine iconography prepares the viewer for Asinou, Lagoudhera, Kykko, St Neophytus and other splendours of the country. Another small church is that of the Panayia Khrysaliniotissa (in Minos Street). This displays a rather wider range of Cypriot icons, from 16th century paintings of the Resurrection and of St Nicholas, incorporating portraits of the donors, to mediocrities of our own day.

Cypriot icon painting reached its zenith in the 11th and 12th centuries and declined swiftly after the 18th century. At the Phaneromeni Church off Ledra Street, the busiest thoroughfare of the inner city, there is a small collection of Cypriot icons, from the 12th to the 16th centuries. Of special merit are a 14th century Virgin and Child, painted on both sides, with the Holy Family's haloes projected in gold relief, and a Dormition, executed in scarlet, blue and gold. But even these are late.

A further introduction to rural arts is provided by the Folk Art Museum which occupies part of the former Archbishop's Palace. Its well ordered collection embraces gourds engraved with religious graphics, fine examples of Lefkara lace-making, robust wooden chests carved with geometric and floral motifs, pottery whose technique and design have barely changed since the bronze age, architectural fragments and a great number of domestic, farming and fishing implements. Suitably, an old woman weaves and embroiders at the entrance.

At the corner of Homer Avenue and Museum Street, in the new city, stands what is surely Nicosia's most interesting building—the Cyprus Museum, founded in 1908 in memory of Queen Victoria, and now the repository of articles from almost every archaeological site in Cyprus. Its proximity to the locations (so often just an hour's ride away), lends it an advantage unshared by the illustrious museums of London, New York and Paris – or even of Athens and Rome. The Museum projects an instant panorama of the island's fertile culture, its versatility and depth of experience, and a visit here is a prerequisite for every field excursion, particularly for such places as Neolithic Khirokitia and bonze age Enkomi where the absence of "dramatic" architecture might otherwise disappoint. From Khirokitia, for instance, one will find a series of terracotta idols whose rounded stylisation seems to anticipate the archaic faces of Cycladic art. From Enkomi comes a remarkable (12th century B.C.) bronze statue of the Horned God (of fertility). From the sanctuary of Ayia Irini near Myrtou, an unforgettable assemblage of some two thousand terracotta votive figures whose sizes range from superman down to five inches. This veritable "village" of clay people indicates the oriental magnificence of the Cypriot kingdoms which, as at Soli and Marium, came within the Egyptian and Persian orbit during the 7th and 6th centuries B.C. The conical head-dress of certain figures resembles the turbans of Achaemenid Persia; their ear-flaps are peculiar to Cyprus. Similar Persianism is discernible in the details of other Cypriot work, for example the horses' feather crests of the great sarcophagus from Amathus, now reposing at New York's Metropolitan Museum.

The collection of bronzes, from the early bronze age to Roman times, shows a similar degree of refinement of execution and animation of spirit to the bronzes of other places, Shang and Chou China, Luristan, Crete, Etruria, Peru and elsewhere. A Cypriot preference for animal subjects like bulls, stags and birds runs parallel with roughly contemporaneous bronze age cultures across the world. Shown too is a rough copper ingot typical of the island's primary export in the Mycenaean period.

From Vounous near Kyrenia (not to be confused with Vouni) there are two clay models of the third millenium, one depicting an agricultural and the other a ritual scene, and each expressed very rhythmically. We find too ritual bowls (2300–2000 B.C.) of clay, having ornament in relief and figures of animals modelled in the round. A wonderful *pyxis* possesses handles representing horses with riders. In technique and inspiration such early Bronze Age pottery suggests Anatolian sources.

An abundance of statuary illustrates the receptivity of the early Cypriots to Egyptian and Graeco-Roman influences. Although few Cypriot sculptors, save Styppax, were renowned in the classical world, sculpture was the island's most popular art till icon painting took over in the Christian era. The Cypriot preferred sculpture in the round to relief carving, except on sarcophagi, probably because stelae and temples were rare in Cyprus. Working in limestone materials that were much softer than Pentelic or Parian marble, and of which there were ample supplies near every city, he used no more than a knife to fashion his art. Cyprian sculpture reached its first peak in the Archaic *kouroi* of the 7th and 6th centuries B.C. and a second in the 4th century B.C. with a number of exquisite limestone heads, many of whch are now unveiled in the Cyprus Museum. Later statuary includes a fine nude sculpture of Aphrodite from Soli (2nd century B.C.), much used today to symbolise Cypriot womanhood and also consumer goods, and a massive Septimus Severus in bronze, unearthed at Kythrea by a farmer's plough. This Roman Emperor, of African extraction, died in A.D. 211, at York.

Not even the briefest inventory of the Museum can neglect mention of the reconstruction of tombs, exhibited downstairs, from successive epochs. The late bronze age tomb sure enough contains Mycenaean pottery. In the Iron Age tomb, at one end of a long *dromos* or passage the human remnants are accompanied by painted vases in the Cypro-Geometric style; at the other end lie the relics of a servant. Characteristically the latest tomb (5th century B.C.) includes pottery imported from Attica. The Museum vaults are stacked with treasures not yet set forth, but a temporary exhibition of recent finds illustrates the field work under way at Enkomi (near Salamis), Salamis itself, Citium (near Larnaca) and Nea Paphos (i.e. lower or New Paphos).

Centuries of looting (for gold and other precious things) once gave the visitor an impression that nothing was left of ancient Cyprus, at Salamis, Soli, Curium and so forth, and it was only when systematic exhumation, as opposed to random rape, was undertaken in the 20th century that the scope of the island's archaeological wealth could be conjectured. The most famous and brazen of early despoilers was General Louis di Cesnola, appointed American Consul by Abraham Lincoln and a founder of the Metropolitan Museum, New York, for which Cyprus was to provide, under his auspices, the nucleus of a collection. In an age (the 1860s to 1870s) when archaeological depredation was at least as respectable as military adventurism, di Cesnola's motives were quite unclouded by artifice. "At the moment of expectation," he wrote, "the excitement of a digger can only be compared with that of a gambler". The General's scholarship luckily matched his energy, and his compendium study *Cyprus, its ancient cities, tombs and temples,* published in 1877, still constitutes basic reading for every archaeologist.

After di Cesnola came the British Museum, whose excavations in the last years of the 19th century helped to swell the national collection in London. But Sir Arthur Evans' discoveries at Knossos deflected interest in favour of Crete and, moreover, as Sir Ronald Storrs put it, "the Cyprus Government was too poor to excavate its own wealth and was prevented by law from allowing anybody else to do so."

Only in 1927 was excavation first undertaken in earnest. A Swedish expedition, financed by the heir to the throne, now King Gustav VI Adolf, set the pioneer pace soon followed all over Cyprus by French, British, American, Canadian, German, Polish and, of course, Cypriot expeditions. The archaeological harvest is still being reaped. Salients have included Professor Schaeffer's confirmation of a Mycenaean link between Enkomi-Alasia and Ras-el-Shamra (Ugarit) in Syria; Dr Dikaios' neolithic digging at Khirokitia and elsewhere, and the continuing work of Professor Karageorghis at Salamis. British visitor to Cyprus is well advised to see the Bri. Museum's new cases entitled "Mycenaean Antiquities froi. Cyprus" (boasting items from Enkomi, Curium, Citium and Marium) and also "Minoan Antiquities from Cyprus". The New Yorker has only to enter the Metropolitan for the bequests of di Cesnola, while the Louvre and Museums of Stockholm and Uppsala are other ideal sources for the study of early Cyprus.

Emerging from the dark calm of the Museum, the eye is dazzled by the midday light. Low buildings of the modern city have the blanched appearance of over-exposed snapshots, but if the *livas* blows, even the heat of summer is bearable. The meridian hours of extended lunch partially relieve the city of its motor traffic, for there is an habitual migration to the hills or beaches, or to the swimming pools which, as at the Hilton and Ledra Palace Hotels, follow a certain routine. In the morning the Danes arrive, athletic and forever somersaulting from the top board, followed by the Anglo-Saxons who rate relaxation higher than splashing. Then maybe a shapely Parisienne in a miniskirt, or a troupe of visiting belly dancers, two of them copper-skinned like Astarte herself, another flopped on the tile like a glistening slug. And the Cypriots? They are lunching at home, at leisure, with grandma and uncle and cousin Nikos invited too. For that is the custom. Poolside meals draw a host of expatriates, and often American cruise tourists in Cyprus "for the day", the retired of Tampa and Tucson, confused about Near Eastern geography and history, but sold on Cyprus.

Afternoon in Nicosia. One drives about the new city and wonders if one will recognise it in five years. Next to the Cyprus Museum gleams the American Center; opposite are an echo of Carnaby Street and a shop for Scandinavian Design. Civic buildings recently encircled by grass are now enmeshed in the plans of government agencies and private investors. On the outskirts have risen the glossy terminal of

Nicosia International Airport (British-financed and German-architected) and at Ayios Dhometios a modern racecourse with Sunday meetings. This is a boom town already possessing the monuments of state, a capital which one hundred years ago contained ten thousand souls (equally divided between Greeks and Turks) and today runs to one hundred thousand. Metaxas Square, the city's hub, flickers with neon slogans for the world's airlines; the Municipal Theatre, a cool Ionic edifice retiring from the street, proffers evenings with the English Chamber Orchestra and the Czech National Ballet; when the moon sizzles through the night haze, one hotel is serving *crevettes Newburg* and *steak au poivre,* another promises "April in Portugal" on an electric harmonica. Government ministers mingle with tourists in the sybaritism of clubs with names like Cosmopolitan, Romantica, Dionysos, Frolics and Key Club. Cinemas, showing many English-language pictures, are the rage.

Manifest poverty is rare in Cypriot cities, especially compared with that encountered in neighbouring countries. After Israel, and before Greece and Turkey, the island has the second highest living standard in the eastern Mediterranean. Cyprus should be proud of its material advances. Ninety per cent of the islanders enjoy the asset of electricity, and illiteracy is now confined to a small and disappearing sector of the rural aged.

How will affluence affect the character of the people? As we have seen, the Cypriots have long assimilated foreign ideas and forms without losing their spiritual identity. In recent years a certain, rather eclectic, effort has been made to preserve traditional arts and festivals and to stimulate curiosity in the past by publicising feats of archaeology, by restoring Byzantine mosaics and frescoes and by examining history. In a land possessing no university (higher education being pursued usually in Greece, England or Turkey), the First International Congress of Cypriot Studies held at Nicosia in 1969 will surely stand out as a landmark on the island's way to knowing itself. On this occasion scholars discussed, with more passion for truth than for *positions prises*, a diversity of topics, including the dialect of Cypriot immigrants in Britain, ancient calligraphy and (a test of faith in academic impartiality) the cultural resemblance between Cypriots and Turks. If Cypriology, one of the world's newer sciences, is to be objective, racial polemics are best avoided.

There is indeed a Cypriot Renaissance, and one of its natural Medici is a daughter of the Paphiot peasantry, Zina Kanther. Married to an American millionaire with holdings in the Cyprus Mining Corporation, she recently acquired in Italy the title Principessa Zina de Tyras and her fame resounds. Not only has she underwritten a modern theatre, a small park and a Cypriot Cultural Centre (near Metaxas Square) for the capital. She has financed several village schools and civic works in the country. And despite a modest formal education, this Cypriot princess displays a literary flair which several graduates of Athens or Salonika might envy. Cyprus lives in Nicosia. A rural pulse thrums not far below the surface. Follow the townspeople into their own clubs and eating places. A fat barman wants to introduce you to Turkish drinking habits. The tavernas throb to the throaty elegiacs of *hassapiko*. Hidden in a palm-fringed villa, the diners at Charlie's Bar feast off monumental *meze* and sing to the bouzouki. Delectable dishes from all of Cyprus are served in the elegant rooms of the Cyprus Tavern while at the Strovolos and Makedonitissa Clubs local wines keep pace with Athenian rhythms.

In their outward aspect Cypriot houses do not show a great variety. In Nicosia and other towns they will possess a flat roof, used for cool sleep in summer. Troodos dwellings, by contrast, have sharply pitched roofs as protection from mountain snow. There, even churches are immured in an outer shell of sloping masonry, giving a distant impression of a big cowshed.

Every newly married Cypriot wishes to own his house and this, like the dowry, is, among conservative families, the bride's responsibility, or rather her father's burden. The mother-in-law issue of the Anglo-Saxon finds a Cypriot parallel in the son-in-law problem as expressed in the Greek aphorism: "whoever has not given birth, whoever has had no house built and whoever has not gone through the expenses of a daughter's wedding knows not the fear of God." The parents of the bride must first decide whether they can afford the price, for the dowry will comprise either material gifts such as a house or a coffer of household goods or, as often today, a cash payment.

In the country the village wedding is a collective effort, particularly for the womenfolk who are responsible for the nuptial feast held on the actual day of the wedding, a Sunday. On the preceding Saturday the priest arrives to bless the bedding, which becomes the object of an ancient ceremony. The priest having departed, a married woman takes the bedding and dances around with it for half a minute. Next it is spread on a mat, and the married women of the bride's family set about re-arranging the wool which is used to stuff the mattress. The woollen strands are now woven in a cruciform pattern symbolic of the Cross and finally the mattress is stuffed at one end with silver coins, is sewn up and "danced" once again, this time by three sturdy village women with a local lad rolled up inside—symbolic of the couple's procreative hopes. The wedding ritual itself provides, in Cyprus as elsewhere, the occasion for piety tempered by merriment, only here there are some special touches. When, for instance, the priest pronounces the solemn words "to love and obey", the bridegroom will step on the bride's toes in emphasis. Lest she forget! At the evening meal the newly married are given a pair of roasted doves—in anticipation of a peaceable partnership.

CHAPTER FOUR

Kyrenia

The road to Kyrenia – Kyrenia Mountains – St Hilarion
castle – Kyrenia: the old city, the castle and its history –
Bellapais Abbey – Buffavento castle – Monasteries of
Antiphonitis, Sourp Magar and St Chrysostom – The forest
road – Kythrea – Zephyros, Pachyammos and Phaliron
beaches – Karavas, Lapithos and Lambousa.

Sixteen miles away the township of Kyrenia curls around its
horseshoe harbour, the most vaunted in Cyprus.

To reach Kyrenia from the capital there is a direct road
north by way of a low gorge in the mountains. After rounding
the grey monument to Atatürk and passing the headquarters
of the Finnish command, the highway threads the straggling
Turkish suburb of Orta Köy to its flag-strewn limits and
savours a first taste of the Cypriot countryside. From February
to May the Mesaoria is bedecked with an extravagance of
flowers, especially the wild poppy. Perhaps nowhere in the
world are the spring flora so prolific as in Cyprus. Beyond
Geunyeli, a Turkish village draped in the national colours
(red and white), the undulating steppe sweeps upwards into
the foothills. There is a wayside restaurant here decorated
in an impossible misunion of colours and adorned with num-
berless mirrors, motley curtains and corrugated screens of
turquoise, each contending for the eye's attention. But the
various products of its kitchen are as ample and luscious a

feast as the imminent landscape. Who would have it otherwise, with for example, the recessed lighting and canned calypso of a bogus ski-lodge? An old man in wide trousers (what the Greeks call *vraka* and the Turks *shalvar*) sits outside and puffs tobacco he has grown himself. He brings water-melons, fresh from the field, when the chef is running short.

The road now straddles the backbone of the Kyrenia Range, skirting first a military kiosk bespangled like a box of candy. Looking back there is a vision of pine-clad pinnacles, a wall of pink limestone scarred by reddish scree and dropping rapidly to the plain. In the far distance, escaping the urban tentacles of Nicosia, the Troodos grandly shout their challenge across the intervening Mesaoria. The two ranges are quite dissimilar. The Kyrenia rises hurriedly from the sea to heights of over three thousand feet. Its sculpted contour has an interesting history, for the great upheavals which formed the Alps and Taurus expended their force by thrusting a wall of limestone against the igneous core of what is now the Troodos Massif. Previously, these limestone beds had lain horizontally some thirty miles north of the present coast of Cyprus, that is in the Caramanian Strait. Several millenia of weather erosion and seismic disturbance had shaped a jumble of heaps, cones and buttes, lending some of them a human aspect. Deep down in hollows and subterranean caverns, natural reservoirs of water, as at Kythrea, have collected, providing a precious resource for the once waterless populations of the southern escarpment. The Kyrenia Range, with its virgin woodlands, appears welcoming from any point.

At the kiosk a lane veers left for the Castle of St Hilarion, which together with the more easterly castles at Buffavento and Kantara, is the stone child of several generations. All three were initiated, in the 11th century, by Alexius I Comnenus and gave Byzantine rulers of the island solid protection against the marauding Arabs. But the Castle of St Hilarion was not so named by its first builders. In Byzantine times it was known as *Didymos* ("Twin") because of the two peaks on which a small monastery associated with the memory of a humble recluse, Hilarion, had been established. In 1191 when Richard Lionheart seized Cyprus, the Fortress of St Hilarion was wrested from the tyrant Emperor Isaac Comnenus by Guy de Lusignan, King of Jerusalem, whose descendants were for three hundred years to use it as a royal residence in summer and a refuge in times of peril.

King Guy hoisted the banners of King Richard on the battlements of the fort, called Didymos, very strongly situated, and exposed on no side to attack; and those who were shut up therein prepared to defend themselves, and for days on end hurled stones and darts at the besiegers, until they were commanded by the Emperor (Isaac) to surrender it; and in it the King placed the Emperor's daughter, lest she be recaptured.

Thus St Hilarion's castle passed under Lusignan rule and was transformed into one of the largest and most impregnable of all Gothic fortresses. In style and spirit it belonged to that great age of castle-building which produced Caernarvon in the west and the Krak des Chevaliers in the east.

St Hilarion consists of three parts, each of which scrambles ever higher up the twin summits. The lower *bourg* comprised an armoury, stables and barracks for infantry and cavalry, but its sheer position, reinforced by Frankish walls, must have rendered even its lower ramparts nearly invulnerable. The middle section was composed of living quarters for the royal entourage. Much of this has been restored to the original plan; it contains a 10th century Byzantine chapel raised on striped pillars, a labyrinth of vaulted chambers divided by a series of arched doorways and, finally, a wood-beamed royal apartment now put to the task of assuaging the visitor's craving for 20th century mineral waters, for the climb is tiring in hot weather. From this refectory the panorama of mountains, sea and forest, framed by the most delicate of stone tracery, is itself a cooling influence, inspiring the sort of romantic imagination which gave the castle a third, Lusignan, name – *Dieudamour*. Or was some erstwhile chevalier unequal to the pronunciation of *Didymos*? St Hilarion Castle was frequently besieged in Frankish days, by dynastic rivals, by the envious Genoese, by famine and pestilence. A contemporary chronicler made mention of an emaciated donkey which provided the starving inhabitants of the castle with their Paschal feast in the year 1230. "They blessed," he writes, "the long-eared lamb, and ate it at Easter." In 1349 the Black Death hit Cyprus with a particular vengeance. Nearly one third of the islanders perished. No remedies were known and the King, Hugh IV, sealed himself up in Dieudamour. Loss of life proved so great among the nobility that he was obliged to fill the depleted peerage by granting baronies to men of the merchant class.

On the highest summit, at 2559 feet, two square towers complete the ensemble. One of them flies the Turkish crescent and from time to time binoculars flash in the sunlight. Ancient monuments have their modern use, or uses. St Hilarion was the castle chosen by Walt Disney for Snow White, and there are, it appears, still Cypriots who like playing "King of the Castle".

The road rolls down the verdant north slope to the plunging seaboard. Theatrically staged around an almost landlocked harbour, the gaunt old houses of Kyrenia gaze northwards to the distant Taurus Mountains of Turkey. *Kerynia* to the Greeks, *Girne* to the Turks, Kyrenia is the loveliest of Cypriot cities and if till recently slow to climb out of its centuries-old shell of lethargy, it now competes, not only in seascapes but also in facilities, with more celebrated spots like Amalfi and Hydra. Its harbour has a frontage much too beautiful to escape entirely the courtship of planners, developers, speculators. These have luckily demonstrated a natural conservatism so that the rather Venetian structures of the front, once peopled by prosperous fisherfolk, have simply been renovated and converted to other uses. First-floor balconies still mark the domestic parts of the house and the lower storeys continue as dépôts, boathouses and shops. An orange awning announces the advent of a discothèque, that *ne plus ultra* of the modern resort. Restaurants and arty little stores have also arrived but retire behind wooden doors and fishing nets. The colours of sea, earth and citrus-grove are picked up again and again in the window shutters and canopies, in the sunshades of waterside cafés and the caïques and yachts at anchor.

Presiding over the scenario, three prominences, castle, minaret and church campanile, symbolise Kyrenia's ancestry. The harbour itself, chanelled between the castle and a long mole marked by lighthouses, affords the best haven on the exposed coast of northern Cyprus. When on occasion wintry winds carry rainclouds over the Strait, this man-made lagoon at Kyrenia is quite still, and you will see kingfishers skimming its surface well before the halcyon days of the winter solstice. Every evening of the warmer seasons the townspeople, who far outnumber tourists, congregate at harbour's edge, to sit alone with a string of worrybeads, to share a jug of reddish *kokkineli* and talk as only Mediterraneans do, to teach small grandchildren how to walk. In the twisting alleys of the town, houses of considerable substance and character cast shadow patterns in the heat of afternoon. Washed in a polychrome range and laced with balconies and belvederes of a striking elegance, the buildings of the town pronounce an unofficial motto of leisure and prosperity.

Though Kyrenia was settled by Achaeans, the relics of its past do not pre-date the Middle Ages, unless we mention the fragments of early churches, used as bollards on the wharf or as capitals for the Byzantine chapel in the castle. Both history and topography are dominated by the fortress which remains to a great extent intact. Its origins are unclear but it appears that the small Byzantine chapel, built in the form of a Greek cross, with its cupola just visible over the fortifications, has the edge of years over the ramparts, walls and bastions which, in restoration, date mainly from the Lusignan and Venetian centuries. After the loss of Acre in 1291, the castle's north and east ranges were totally rebuilt and a massive new wall added to the south. Its redoubled strength commended it for use as a state prison. In 1310 several nobles who had supported the usurper to the Lusignan throne (of Henry II) were confined to its *oubliettes*, "very dark and horrible", the Prince of Galilee by himself and the others in pairs, to die a lingering death by starvation. Others followed, among them Jeanne Laleman, mistress of Peter I incarcerated during his absence by Queen Eleanor, whose jealousy provoked the most elaborate tortures. Jeanne's tragedy is still commemorated in the Cypriot folk-song of Arodaphnousa. A few years later the fort successfully staved off the Genoese, who had already taken Famagusta and Nicosia, and in 1426 the Regent took refuge from the Mamelukes, together with the royal family and their treasure.

Kyrenia was again besieged in 1460, when James the Bastard usurped the throne from his step-sister Charlotte and the latter repaired to the castle with her supporters. While James mounted cannon on the roof of a neighbouring church and enlisted the aid of Mameluke mercenaries, the castle's own artillery withheld his attacks for four years, in which extremity its occupants were reduced to a diet of dogs, cats and vermin. It was the Venetians who adapted the fortress for the more lethal warfare of the Renaissance. They added massive towers with gun-emplacements and in 1560 erected a stern rectangular bastion at the south-western corner. Ten years later, their work came to a halt when the fortresses were surrendered on the first demand of the Turkish admiral, so disheartened were the garrison by the news of the fall of Nicosia. Under British occupation, the castle was used first as a prison and then, till 1950, as a police barracks. During the Emergency it served as a place of internment for EOKA fighters, some of whom engineered daring escapes. Even today there is a military function, for units of the *Kypriakon*

Navtikon or Cypriot Navy are stationed here and the Hellenic standard flutters proudly from the entrance.

See the dungeons. Some of these are lit by diminutive slits overlooking the sea; from here the prisoner gazed on the tantalising movement of ships in the harbour. Other cells are buried deep in the bowels of the building, either immured in the limestone masonry or else hewn straight from the rock. An occasional shaft admits a piercing speck of sunlight but as a rule the gloom is unrelieved. The Crusaders Tower at the north-eastern angle has, by contrast, a spacious upper chamber whose chinks give on to green eddies of tide and the reef-like mole of the harbour. Torpedo-boats, by no means an anachronism, are moored alongside. From the summit of this tower, which is the castle's highest vantage point, the view envelops a semi-circle of sea, the serpentine fall and rise of the Anatolian mainland and the Gothic silhouette of the mountainous backdrop to Kyrenia itself, with the perpendicular bulk of Bellapais Abbey and the airy turrets of St Hilarion and Buffavento foremost. At the castle's foot, the fragile minaret of the Jafer Pasha Mosque, damaged in the troubles of 1963 but now restored, reminds us of Kyrenia's Muslim population. It may be that animals running loose below the battlements are holding their chivalric games: two horned rams, for instance, contesting their primacy over a flock of awed females, each ram withdrawing backwards ten yards before advancing to meet, with a resounding crack, its adversary. Human warfare must, in comparison, have sent a shiver down the entire mountain spine. Offshore, perhaps a mile away, there is further activity. Archaeologists of the University of Pennsylvania are diving ninety feet to a Greek ship wrecked in the 4th century and supposedly laden with riches.

All along the coastal outskirts of Kyrenia new villas and honeymoon cottages announce the terms of some far away entrepreneur. The Kyrenia of the 1930s was an exclusive retreat for the very retired and rather refined. The British in particular, for whom sunshine and low taxes are an irresistible combination, made it their home. There was a certain English lady who on Saturdays presented every member of the populace with a florin. An offshore island known to this day, quite inappropriately, as the "Island of Snakes" took its name from a misogynist clergyman who strongly resented the nerve of the Englishwomen sunbathing, "like reptiles", in a state of complete undress. Motor traction was limited to three taxis and it was more usual to approach Bellapais by mule, halting frequently for shade under a carob tree.

Some of the spirit of pre-war Kyrenia lingers on, for Cyprus, spacious and distant as it is, has not yet felt the intemperate force of the tourist revolution, for which we must be grateful. Looking as though uprooted from the Cyclades, the little Church of St Andrew, with its red tiles and walls as white as sea-foam, caters to a community of Anglicans. A more recent patroness of Cypriot arts and sciences, Lady Loch of Ayios Epiktitos, has donated a harbour-side house, containing her collection of folk art, to the Antiquities Department. She has supported too a definitive study entitled *Birds of Cyprus*. Nonetheless beneath the "Tree of Idleness" at Bellapais, Dimitri's café, immortalised in Lawrence Durrell's *Bitter Lemons*, has been reconstructed and it is ironical that whilst the Anglo-Cypriots are vocal conservationists, loth to accept any change in this small corner of an earthly paradise, the villagers favour all manner of innovation. Durrell, who lived in Bellapais till the Troubles began, understood Cyprus a good deal better than most of his compatriots, and *Bitter Lemons*, basically sympathetic to the islanders, opens windows on the Cypriot mind.

Bellapais, five miles uphill from Kyrenia, is the perfect Greek arrangement of houses staggering uphill, of arcaded balconies encompassing the bluish sweep of the orange and lemon plantations and the unruffled sheet of water separating Cyprus from Asia Minor. The sounds of the afternoon commingle, a braying donkey, the tintinnabulation of goats

62

Selimiye Mosque, Nicosia,
originally built in the 13th century as St Sophia Cathedral

overleaf: Kyrenia

devouring another shrub, the coffee-house chatter of men beneath the tree with the lime-washed trunk. Fortunately newer houses conform to the old styles, witness Ambelia which, with its neat balustrades, white stucco and heavy shutters, is advertised in the London press as an incipient Cypriot village, enhanced by a swimming-pool and improved plumbing.

But Bellapais, whose very name derives from the Latins, is nothing without its Abbey, founded in 1206 and now probably the supreme instance of Frankish architecture in the Near East. Its church, adapted to the Orthodox rite and endearingly cluttered with an assortment of chairs, pews and tapers for the faithful, possesses the main features of 13th century Gothic but their effect is modified by the Greek iconostasis added in 1884, to the right of which is an opening, now blocked, whereby lepers could attend services. Less altered is the 14th century cloister. With its ogival arches, flamboyant tracery and its corbels wonderfully carved in human, animal and floral shapes, this is a pure translation of the Gothic spirit to the Near East. Unlike the Norman churches of Sicily which were strongly infused with the Islamic spirit of the Saracens, Frankish Bellapais makes no stylistic concessions either to the preceding cultures of Cyprus or to those Arab models of the Levant which were well known to the Crusaders. In all likelihood it is the luxuriance of local greenery and the drama of what Durrell calls the "Gothic Range" – the chain of hills rising from the village – which give this mellow export of the Catholic north a compelling appropriateness.

The chapter-house, where the canons took their places every morning to deal with routine matters of church management, is now only a husk of its former self but one may still climb its staircases, and from its terraces observe mediaeval building techniques laid bare by the loss of its roof. Most of the sculpted corbels of the latter still stand : Daniel fighting with two wild animals, Ulysees flanked by sirens, a monkey and a cat intwined in a pear-tree. Finally there is the refectory, now as elegant in the restoration of its rib-vaulted roof, its ogival arches, trefoils and east rose window, as in the 13th century when Hugh III lent his royal patronage to the white-haired Premonstratensian brethren whose order had originated at Laon. This exquisite six-bay chamber, like the Abbey itself, grew derelict in the 15th and 16th centuries as the monks indulged in such profligate delights as the maintenance of three wives a-piece. The Turks, as was their custom, encouraged Orthodox worship in place of the Latin and consequently the church alone continued to flourish. The Abbey's lowest degradation came, surely, in the early years of our century when the refectory operated as a miniature rifle range for the instruction of British troops. The windows are still deprived of glass, with the happy result that in the evening shrilling swallows trace figures of eight under the groin vaults of the ceiling.

The Abbey is the property of the Department of Antiquities and it is lovingly tended by a remarkable custodian. Kostas Kollis, who wears a rogue's expression, is a man with a golden heart and the greenest of fingers. The four small cypress trees which he planted in 1940 are now towering landmarks of the Kyrenia shore. They shoot from a cloister garden ablaze with Mediterranean flora. The genus cypresses (*kyparissos* in Greek), holds, by the way, no etymological relation to the island's name. Just inside the main gate thrives a magical tree bearing both oranges and lemons, and the farther one walks the more outsanding are the species. Roses of velvety white and vinous red cohabit one and the same bush, and in a secluded nook near the cloister nine varieties of nut, peach, cherry and plum, all issuing from a shrub which started life as an almond-tree, confront the disbelieving eye. Mr. Kollis is wont to perform his miracles in May, for that is the season most propitious for grafting unless—be it noted—clouds fill the sky or the Anatolian *livas* is blowing strong. The custodian of Bellapais knows as much about Cyprus as anybody in Kyrenia, and more than most. His office is not merely a museum of pennants, penknives and postage-stamps but the obvious destination for all who seek counsel, and also amusement. There was lately an American lady of a credulous nature who, when assured that "next year bananas will appear on the cherry tree", promised to come again, with her camera. From Bellapais well-beaten paths climb upwards to Buffavento Castle, the Gothic sentinel which keeps one guardian eye on the northern coast, and another on the Mesaoria. We shall come shortly to Buffavento, by an easier way.

Kyrenia lies in the middle of a riviera celebrated for its winter mildness and rich flora. The farther one travels, especially eastwards, along the shoreline the more devoid of habitation it becomes, and many of its beaches are quite deserted every day of the year. This is not true, however, of the sandy bays huddling closest to Kyrenia, in particular Phaliron and Pachyammos ("Thick Sand") for those have been discovered by the tourist, by Cypriot townspeople and UN servicemen and their families, all devotees of ultra-violet. Phaliron is the more sheltered when the wind blusters across from Asia Minor, whipping the sea into flecks of whiteness. Behind, a phalanx of scrub oak and olives recedes to the hinterland. More reminiscent of the Cretan littoral, Pachyammos is trimmed with sand-dunes, tall grass and sporadic encampments of khaki and orange tents flapping in the sea-wind. On these beaches, indeed all round the island's coast, the balm of the sea breeze can delude the novitiate sunbather into underestimating the burning force of the sunshine: at least on the first roasting.

Eastward the road, metalled but narrow, winds relentlessly along the indentations of a battered, scarce visited coast. Now and then a diminutive chapel crouches low among the sea-sprayed rocks. Tiny white shrines – boxes with glass doors for devotional candles – help define the roadside for night travellers. A lone *kafeneion*, washed in pastel shades, advertises America's favourite refreshment. Though practically unpopulated, the countryside is carefully tilled, and a profusion of wild flowers, red, yellow, orange, pink and blue, fills those parts left untrammelled by the scythe and plough. By turning south through the scattered village of Ayios Amvrosios, it is possible to cross the mountains to Nicosia or else to proceed down the Forest Road, which exists as an auxiliary to the reforestation of the hillsides, but rivals the most famous panoramic highways in the grandeur of landscape. Ayios Amvrosios recalls one of those archetypal villages appearing in the films of Cacoyannis, *Elektra, Antigone, Zorba*. Peppers and tobacco hang from sun-bleached eaves of cedar-wood; the village patriarchs, heavily whiskered and clad in black sashes and *vraka*, fill the stage of their cavernous door-steps while the black-hooded women play the unwitting role of chorus. Michael Cacoyannis is Cypriot by origin and followed in his youth a customary route to success in the Hellenic world, from Nicosia to London where he was a war-time broadcaster in the Greek service of the BBC, finally to Athens to become in the 1950s, the doyen of Greek cinematographers.

By zig-zags the mountain road ascends the coniferous crest of the Kyrenia Mountains. Half-hidden in a fold of the wooded mountainside, the mellow sandstone walls of Antiphonitis church – a 12th century octagon supporting a simple, spacious dome – outlives the monastery of which it once was part. In March and April the church's precincts are carpeted with marigolds; in its courtyard a green copper bell is slung from a bough, and fig-trees abound on the fringe of a gurgling spring. Of great interest are the interior frescoes, most dating from the late 15th century except for a few 12th century paintings in the bema (sanctuary), the apse and south-west corner of the naos (nave). Unusual is the two-dimensional effect of a series of figures (prelates, deacons, martyrs) painted on the church's eight rounded piers. The pictorial and architectural qualities of Antiphonitis are doubtless heightened by the seclusion of its natural setting, and those who visit it share the joy of contemplation with its founders.

Mounting the saddle of the easternmost range behind Antiphonitis, we face a fantastic scenery of deep ravines, of boulders set at vertiginous angles and evergreens of a thousand shades. Dark gorges wind to the chalky cliffs that arch the northern coastline. Like flags pinned on a school atlas for the instruction of children, tall lean belfries mark village settlements in the plain. Veering west again along the ridge we enter the Forest Road. Though unmetalled, its width and the firmness of its red earth are adequate even in the wet season, and there is virtually no motor traffic or, indeed, any human presence to interrupt the silence. Out to the west the peaks of Pentadactylos, Buffavento and St Hilarion march in a regular concatenation till they recede into haze. Beyond the shore, where the sea has bitten elliptical chunks from the land, we can scan the strait as far as the continental Taurus. The conifers flourishing in this great forest display little regimentation, and wild life thrives unhindered. Sometimes scurrying into an undergrowth strewn with fir-cones, the francolin (or black partridge) reminds us of its survival on the island. Once a favourite game bird, the francolin – which makes most of Asia its habitat and is still prolific in the tea plantations of India – was till the 1950s almost hunted to extinction. The firearms prohibition of the Emergency happily released it from such a fate, and it is today a Protected Creature. With its black chest, spotted feathers and bright chestnut collar, the male of the species is particularly fine.

As the highway nears Halevka, a hill retreat with hotels, camping and tennis courts among the trees, the arid southern side of the mountains opens up. Here the threadbare flanks drop sharply to the Mesaoria, the sparseness of their vegetation contrasting with the munificence bestowed by nature on the northern side. A by-road near Halevka, marked with a signpost, turns off for the Armenian Monastery of Sourp Magar, which sits in a cleft of the northern slopes overlooking the sea. Its clergy, its services and inscriptions are a reminder that the Turks do not constitute the sole minority in Cyprus, for Armenians, Maronites, Jews and gypsies also have an historic place. The Monastery was till 1425 a Coptic settlement, then handed over to the Armenian colony. After the Armenian Massacres of the years 1895–97, when dismembered corpses were said to have floated across the Strait from Anatolia, this monastery was put to use as an orphanage for young Armenian fugitives from Ottoman terror. Nowadays the severity and desolation of its reconstruction are relieved once a year, on the first Sunday of May, when Armenian Cypriots congregate here to honour their saint.

Ahead sprout the five fingers of the Pentadactylos (3131 feet) which, together with an island near Vouni and a rock at Paphos, is forever linked to the memory of Akritas Dighenis, legendary defender of Cyprus from the Arabs, in the eighth and ninth centuries. In hot pursuit of the Saracen invaders, Dighenis left here, as he vaulted over the mountains, the huge imprint of his heroic hand. "Of Greek father and Oriental mother," says Kazantzakis, Dighenis is "the symbolic hero of the race," that is of all Greeks. In our own time his patriotic energy was emulated by George Grivas "Dighenis" who led EOKA in their guerrilla war against the British. The General is now retired in Greece but the archives and exhibits of the small Museum of Cypriot Resistance at Nicosia (Larnaca Street) illustrate the trials and victories of his career.

The eastern Forest Road has lately been extended beyond the monoliths of the Pentadactylos in the direction of Buffavento, whence it joins the western highroad of the same name. At the end of a short cul-de-sac a stony track climbs to three thousand feet past lichen-covered rocks and cone-laden pines to the Castle of Buffavento, crowning one of the titans of the chain. The peerless spectacle radiating from what was once a Byzantine look-out and then a Frankish fortress embraces not only the green-and-white mosaic of Kyrenia just below, but also the dorsal summits which vanish on the stone panhandle of the remote Karpas. On the south side Famagusta, Nicosia and the Troodos are grey on the plain; dust-clouds spiral from tile quarries in the foothills and irrigation lakes sparkle like deep-set eyes. The castle itself is the scene of active restoration. On a flat roof scarved women sift through lumps of earth in search of Frankish treasures. A transistor wireless emits Greek music of the *laiki* sort, lending rhythm to their labours. Only in 1969 was a custodian appointed to Buffavento. Sightseers arrive, but in small numbers, perhaps because the hardship of the ascent is much exaggerated. Known in late Byzantine days as *Spitia tis Reginas* ("Queen's Lodgings"), after a half-legendary Cypriot queen who maintained one hundred and one "houses" or chambers (of which one remains a secret to this day), Buffavento was so called by its Lusignan occupants who not infrequently found the summit to be "buffeted by the wind". Using local materials the Franks built upper and lower wards, each of which follows the contour of its rocky base. These have lain in ruins since Venetian occupation—even if in 1570 many citizens of Nicosia took refuge in them during the Ottoman siege. Historically its extreme height and solitariness commended it less to fortification than to imprisoning political and dynastic foes. A Kafkaesque setting inspired a whole inventory of subtle torturings within its walls and the cries of its victims must have gone unheard, save by the eagles having their eyries in the rock.

At one turn of the road which twists down the mountainside there appears of a sudden the Monastery of Ayios Chrysostomos, a walled oasis of cypresses and orange-trees in which repose the contiguous churches of St Chrysostom and the Holy Trinity. The former was rebuilt in 1891 in a modified form of the original basilica. Its iconostasis and newer icons exhale an air of *fin de siecle,* although a majestic, wood-carved, west door and a number of respectable wall icons (including an Archangel) remain from the 12th century. The Church of the Holy Trinity, on the other hand, is now convincingly renovated in the spirit of its Byzantine founder, one Philocales Eumathius who probably dedicated it in the year 1110, when the preponderance of Constantinople dictated an extensive use of brick and a highly refined style of wall painting. The frescoes of this church, probably the work of a painter trained in Constantinople, has been restored in egg tempera by the same team from the Dumbarton Oaks Institute which revivified the painted interior of the church at Lagoudhera (Chapter 5) and completed similar tasks at Asinou (Chapter 5) in Cyprus, also in Serbia, Trebizond and, in Istanbul, at Kariye Jami and the greatest church of eastern Christendom, St Sophia, now a museum. The Church of the Holy Trinity boasts a few pictorial masterworks, especially four figures – each named for a different Gregory – on the walls of the north-west recess, but the monastery's chief spiritual asset is its splendid other-worldliness, the more profound when one stops to consider the clamorous pace of Nicosia recumbent in the plain. In the cloisters a source of mountain water gushes forth; thereby hangs the story of the monastery's origins – there is hardly a monastery in Cyprus without an extraordinary genesis. Not far away a Byzantine princess, who is buried *in situ* with two of her slaves, once sought asylum from the Templars. It seems that she was afflicted with an ulcer complaint. Her little dog, which had previously never left her side, soon contacted a similar ailment and would vanish for long intervals every day, returning home in better health as time wore on. It was seen to bathe in the small spring which we have mentioned, and having tried the remedy for herself, its royal mistress was fast cured and, in token of her gratitude, founded the Monastery.

It is eleven miles from here to Nicosia, by way of a dry wasteland and foothills wounded by quarrying. At Mia Milea we can instead go east to Kythrea, whose riotous greenery and orangeries testify to another source of water, or *kephalovryso*, whose beneficence became less startling only when large-scale irrigation was introduced on the Mesaoria. In legend the spring at Kythrea was forced by hydraulic pressure from the Taurus Mountains of Asia Minor and channelled below the sea through some miraculous duct. In Roman times its water was borne by aqueduct to Salamis (then called Constantia). All mediaeval attackers laying siege to Nicosia were obliged first of all to take Kythrea, capturing in particular the flour-mills driven by its famous stream. The common cauliflower, first brought to Europe in 1604, is native to this handsome village and today cactus, palms, olives and fruit-trees jostle one another in ordered exuberance. The southern slopes of the Kyrenia Range are, moreover, tangibly warmer than the maritime, and at well-watered Kythrea the grazing land is very fertile, as may be guessed from the symphony of goat bells often heard in the village streets as gaunt old women drive their flocks and herds from one rich pasture to another.

Before leaving the area under survey one should return to Kyrenia and now head westwards, past the Five-Mile Beach and Golden Rock Beach, both exposed to commercial winds, and beyond the pottery village of Ayios Yeoryios to the sandy bay at Zephyros, named for the God of the West Wind. On its promontory, alfresco dishes of *dolmadhes, keftedhes* and other Greek perennials are offered in a pleasant restaurant and except on holidays there is seldom a crowd to spoil the privacy of Zephyros. Larks soar in the sky, and well into early summer the faraway Taurus wears caps of snow. Beyond the beach, and connected to the main highway by a lane, one of the best hotels of the north coast, the Mare Monte, rises from its sequestered cove, with a fleet of canoes and catamarans plying their bathing-suited passengers to rocks and islets otherwise inaccessible.

Eight miles west of Kyrenia the road narrows at the big village of Karavas. Citrus groves spreading from here to modern Lapithos are so valuable that their proprietors have thus far resisted the demand of central authority for widening and straightening the highway. The motorist will smile again after Lapithos when his vehicle reasserts its tyranny on a surprisingly broad road edging round the western end of the hills and, avoiding as it does the Turkish-populated lands,

71

takes the bulk of the Greek Cypriot traffic between Kyrenia and the capital. Close to the coast near Karavas is Lambousa, site of an older Lapithos, originally settled by Laconians from the Peloponnese and now yielding a wealth of ancient treasures, including some unusual early Christian silver bowls depicting the life of David. The name Lambousa means "shining" and this is a fitting epithet for the culture that once grew on its shores. Nowadays the disused Monastery of Akhiropiitos, with a large church dating principally from the 12th century, the nearby rock-hewn Chapel of Ayios Evlambios and the 15th century Church of Ayios Evlavios, perched above the sea, are melancholy mementoes of greatness, sad warnings of the changes which may befall whole cities. The modern Lapithos, a large village that hogs a lot of tourist literature, is actually made of masonry robbed from the seaside monuments of its predecessor. Like Kythrea it owes its famous welfare to a *kephalovryso* bursting from a rock nearly one thousand feet up, and bringing to fruition myriad lemons and mulberries on the side of the mountain. In such places where the "hydraulic society" is so dependent upon the concentrated availability of water, the theories of Oriental Despotism expounded by Karl Wittfogel, make ringing sense. Control of water resources, whether of the Nile or Indus, of a Saharan *wadi* or the bubbling springs on an island without lakes and permanent rivers, has historically been a key to power in Asia and Africa. However, in Cyprus, the despotism was generally foreign.

CHAPTER FIVE

Morphou

Myrtou and Ayia Irini – Morphou – Oranges and lemons –
Xeros and Lefka – Mining industries – Vouni Palace and the
Theatre of Soli – The Kokkina coastline – Peristerona –
Asinou Church – Lagoudhera.

For centuries, palaces and pleasure domes prosper on the
wealth of fertile lands, on mineral abundance and trade with
distant countries. Then of a sudden the lights go out. Trade
recedes and the cities are left high and dry, disinherited even
by the peasants who use them as a stone quarry. Their
memorials pine for the explorer-scholar whose pleasure it is
to reassemble an ancient configuration. Paestum and Paly-
myra, Ctesiphon and Chichen Itza are thus reclaimed, for the
eternal benefit of dilettanti and charabanc parties. Representative of this rule are the relics of those early Cypriot cultures
which were hemmed in on the north and west by the Bay
of Morphou, for they too retreated into the dunes. The
traditional industry of the region, namely copper mining,
languished for long periods, to be fully revived only within
our own century. Hence the great monuments of Vouni and
Soli at one end of the bay and the excavations of Ayia Irini
at the other, pose unanswered questions as to why their
brilliant epochs came so swiftly to grief and why they had
no successor settlements.

The Morphou area is, however, again swept by a spring tide

of success. Not only do the copper mines of Mavrovouni and Skouriotissa furnish the country with its most valuable single asset, but the town of Morphou itself is the headquarters of a fast expanding citrus cultivation. From an incoming aeroplane one sees the orange plantations march in regiments towards the inland plateau, the vineyards creep up the grey watercourse towards Mount Olympus, the mine-working scoured from the reddish foothills.

On the ground, a northern approach from Lapithos (Chapter 4) rounds the Kyrenia Range, loops through glacial valleys of ravishing fecundity and then divides near the village of Myrtou. Eastwards is Nicosia, at the end of a highway taking in the mesa formations of the plain and a scattering of small towns (Asomatos, Kondemenos, Skylloura) each of which is distinguished by a tall white church. Southwards is Myrtou, pleasantly rural. Its Church of Ayios Panteleimon once formed the kernel of a monastery. Today housing units of the National Guard, the monastery walls are bespattered with blue slogans on the *enosis* theme, and soldiers will show the visitor around the church. Though crude, it has coloured windows which project kaleidoscopic refractions on the icons, and a curious semi-circular panel showing an idealised picture of the after-life. Near Myrtou, on the turning to Cape Kormakiti, is a village, Kormakiti, of Maronites, members of that eastern Christian sect based in the Lebanon and descendants of a Cypriot Maronite colony which in the Middle Ages numbered no less than sixty villages. Now, after centuries of marriage into Greek Orthodox families, their strength is reduced to some three thousand, settled in four villages. Maronites own most of the camels remaining in Cyprus.

Another track branches off for Ayia Irini where the Swedish Expedition of 1929 fell upon the extraordinary terracottas happily exhibited in the Cyprus Museum. We do not know the name of the original settlement but it is clear that it attained its peak in the late 6th and early 5th centuries B.C., in decades of indirect rule from Assyria and Egypt. The sands of time are more than a rhetorical allusion to the subsequent history of Ayia Irini, for the dunes steadily devoured its precincts and surrounding meadow until their encroachment was stemmed in recent years by afforestation. Nowadays the terrain is fruitful and in the right season the floor is interspersed with wild lilies.

While without any claim to classical or mediaeval magnificence, Morphou is the natural centre of north-western Cyprus. The 15th century Church of Ayios Mamas is an exemplary marriage of the Byzantine and Gothic styles and it contains a fine iconostasis influenced by Venetian painting. It is the popular belief that the sarcophagus of St Mamas, who was martyred by the Turks in Pamphylia, was cast out to sea, whence it floated across the strait to a position offshore from Morphou. There on the same night, the saint appeared to one of the villagers and ordered him to bear the coffin to land. In some trepidation the villager set out with his sons and a team of four oxen, to find the waters parting before them and revealing the sarcophagus. The oxen then drew it as far as the village where it refused to go further. Thinking this to be a signal of the saint's wishes, the Morphiots at once built a church to house his mortal remains, naming it in his honour.

Throughout the year citrus fairly bulges in the leafy dark orchards of this region. After harvesting, oranges, lemons and grapefruit are heaped in pails at the roadside and they are more remarkable for having been introduced to Morphou only in 1930. Mediaeval visitors noted orangeries in Famagusta, Lapithos and Lefka but passed over Morphou. An Italian traveller observed in 1760 "cotton, silk, grain and sugar cane, due to the abundance of water" but made no mention of fruit. In 1879 the quotable Baker depicted Morphou as dusty, arid and dry in summer, a swamp in winter. It had houses of sun-baked bricks of clay and broken straw, fruitful gardens irrigated by water-wheels and a rich sandy loam which had formerly produced madder roots. But Morphou now had "to depend upon silk and cereals for its agricultural wealth". As a consequence of its new occupation, a building boom is in progress. The residences of a confident class of entrepreneurs, as substantial as Alpine farmhouses, shoot up in gardens of mimosa and sunflowers. Modern appliances grace every kitchen, and blue cylinders for water storage crown each roof.

The principal mining zone of Cyprus lies to the west. At Pendayia ("Five Saints") the Cyprus Mines Corporation crushing plant is seen, a long low lateral edifice. Nearby, the United States owners have installed a workers' hospital and a golf course. Golf is not yet a national pastime. Into the broad Bay of Morphou the River Marathasa debouches its wintry torrent and here the earth is a glowing incarnadine. Soil, water and climate collaborate to make Xeros and Lefka a subtropical pocket. The island's fattest palms, banana-trees and cactus line the lower flanks of the mountains while the upper reaches are clothed with mighty pines. The township of Lefka, in particular, is engulfed by the foliage of gardens and orchards. Elm and ash, maples, poplars and numerous fruit trees shade the environs. Lefka is a predominantly Turkish town, as one cannot but notice by the standards blazing from the rooftops. At the mines down the road, man-made mountains of copper pyrites – the *aes cyprium* worked by Phoenicians, Romans and Americans – proclaim the pigment red, so that modern copper excavation is far more cheerful than the dreary earthworks defacing the pleasant lands of Yorkshire or West Virginia. Ore is extracted by the C.M.C. at Mavrovouni and at Skouriotissa ("Our Lady of the Slag") whence it is carried by company railway to the port of Xeros. Here the cupreous effluent mingles in the sea with natural shades of aquamarine. A conveyor jetty with automatic loader lunges seawards to meet the ore-ships; tugs and lighters are ranged offshore while onward down the coast, beyond Vouni, a wall of steep mountains fills the western extremity of Morphou Bay.

Mineral wealth is exploited at other places in the island. The Hellenic Mining Company excavates copper at Kalavassos in the south and chrome from the northern flanks of Mount Olympus. At Limni on Khrysokhou Bay, the Cyprus Sulphur and Copper Company is busy extracting pyrites from open-cast quarries, while at Amiandos, in the central Troodos, asbestos is worked by Cyprus Asbestos Mines. For all this activity the island possesses no industrial towns as such and its landscape is little disfigured by the slag-heaps, cranes and chimneys of more and less fortunate countries.

West of Xeros nature again excels herself in the splendour of settings. According to Herodotus, the first known kingdom to embrace these shores was Aepia, which Solon the lawgiver visited on a voyage from Egypt to Athens. Solon, it appears, was so taken with the beauty of the place now called Soli, after him, that he persuaded Philocyprus, the King of Aepia, to transfer thither his capital, while the great Athenian prolonged his sojourn in the role of an early town-planning consultant. Plutarch has expressed Solon's hopes:

> If in the scenes to her so justly dear,
> My hand a burgeoning city helped to rear,
> May the sweet voice of smiling Venus bless
> And speed me home with honours and success.

Thus Soli became one of the ancient realms of Cyprus, and in 498 B.C. rallied to the Ionians in their revolt against Persia, being subject to a five-month siege. It later declared for Alexander the Great and reached the peak of its fortune under the Romans who, in the 2nd century A.D., endowed it with an open-air auditorium, lately restored to its original condition. The Swedes discovered the theatre in 1930, together with a temple of Aphrodite and a superb Hellenistic marble statue of the goddess, now safe in the Cyprus Museum.

Atop a conical hill which dives straight into the sea, neighbouring Vouni occupies probably the most evocative situation

77

in Cyprus. Row upon row of little peaks, dotted with carob and olive trees and carved with furrows, hem the sparkling coast towards Kokkina Point. In the other direction the smiling Bay of Morphou sweeps the feet of the Kyrenia hills. But the history of Vouni is largely mysterious. Probably thriving in the 5th century B.C. its earliest architecture and artefacts suggest an oriental impact and thus a political preference for Persia during the Ionian Rebellion. It may have been a satellite of Marium (the modern Polis tis Khrysokhous farther west) which itself was Persophile until the Athenian General Cimon captured it in 449 B.C. and established a new pro-Greek dynasty there, which helps explain the transformation of the main palace and the appearance of a Temple of Athena today – thanks to the work of the Swedish Expedition – evident at Vouni. The new dynasty probably controlled Vouni for some seventy years, till fire destroyed the palace (*c.* 380 B.C.). Soon afterwards a *coup de grâce* may have been delivered by Soli, which now leaned towards Persia and doubtless mistrusted its rival. On its three levels the remains of the palace define most clearly the original layout, which provided kitchens and bathing arrangements to an unusual extent, for one is struck by the elaboration of the baths : the caldarium, frigidarium and sudatorium, the latter set off by a fine pointed arch of a kind seen (perhaps in the Cypriot memory) at Mycenae. Although pink limestone is much used at Vouni there are walls of original mud brick whose manufacture today differs but little from the ancient formula. It should be stated, however, that Cypriot bricks, being notably thinner and lighter than the traditional brick of Aegean and mainland Greece, resemble more closely the ancient mode of Anatolia. In the main court, once covered by a peristyle portico, a stone stele, resembling a fiddle-shaped female figure of Cycladic art, rises alone from the courtyard. Far from being a human representation, this is in fact an uncompleted windlass for use with the cistern next to it.

Buffavento Castle

The Abbey at Bellapais

Peristerona

Few travellers today proceed along the rocky coast beyond
Vouni and the red island of Petra tou Limniti, which Dighenis
is said to have cast at the Saracens. Certainly the road de-
teriorates, and villages encountered on the way are quite
aggressively either Greek or Turkish strongholds, for the
respective flags adorn many a mountain top. But Irish patrols
from the UN keep the peace, and for the more audacious
driver the winding road to Polis, by way of Kokkina ("Red")
and Pomos Points, is constantly rewarding. This is Tylliria,
and its hills and headlands descend to a narrow coast of a
grandeur seldom equalled, to rivermouth villages like Kato
Pyrgos half-drowned in plantations of banana and citrus, to
cliff-hanging villages like Pomos, whose houses of sun-baked
earth and brick blend with the background. The scenery to
the left is a wild mass of mountains, cut by deep and dark
ravines, while the florid cliffs, reminiscent of Devon, are in
places carved by human hand so that wheat ripens on parallel
shelves of rich red soil. A series of promontories carries the
north-western spurs of the Troodos to the brink. Mountain
roads thread up some of the valleys to Stavros tis Psokas and
the Monastery of Kykko but they are only passable in fine
weather, and in no case do they promise a rapid return to
Nicosia.

Inland from Morphou Bay the Mesaoria is bounded by the
hulking massif of the northern Troodos. An agreeable village,
Peristerona, crouches in the foothills. With its domed church
and mosque often invoked as symbols of the place's racial
harmony, Peristerona also has a simple symmetry in its buildings and its daily life. The five-domed church is modelled on
the prototype of the Coronation Church of the Apostles at
Constantinople and is named for St Barnabas and St Hilarion,
not the obvious saints but rather two 5th century Cappadocian
soldiers who became friars. Built long after the advent of the
Latins, it testifies to the enduring spirit of Byzantium. Only
two other Cypriot churches, at Emba and Yeroskipos, both
near Paphos, follow a similar plan. In its iconostasis there is

a beautiful 16th century icon of Christ's Presentation in the Temple. Though there is no attempt at perspective, the figures here (especially those of the women), amount to portraiture rather than iconography and the whole work, and the serenity of its style, recalls the best of Sienese painting. Also in the church reposes a crude old chest with a painted lid, expressive of a robust and primitive eloquence.

Entrenched higher up in the hills two of the outstanding monuments of Byzantine creation can be seen. These are the churches at Asinou and Lagoudhera, whose resplendent frescoes have but lately come to the world's attention. To reach the former there are two routes from Peristerona. One pursues the Peristerona Valley and is used mainly by diesel lorries trundling back and forth from quarries in the hills. As the valley deepens, the tidy plots of the small farmer give way to a sparse forest. The second approach is to pass Astromeritis on the highroad from Nicosia to Troodos and then to fork left at Kato Koutraphas up the little dale of the Elea. At the ramshackle village of Nikitari the mild priest must be roused from his white-washed house and his company sought if one wishes to enter the glorious church known as Panayia tis Asinou or Panayia Phorbiotissa. For he possesses the key.

There was once at this spot a city named Asine after the Argolid city of the Peloponnese whence settlers arrived in the 11th century B.C., but nothing remains of it. Indeed the little church now stands alone among fertile hills and forest. Its outer walls and roof, designed to protect the interior from the wrath of winter, seem so unmonumental that one might pass it by in ignorance. The priest throws its doors wide open, letting in the light and bumble bees and animating the still pageant of its frescoes, which cover all the walls. The paintings, set within red margins against mainly ultramarine background, have both a pictorial intensity and an urgent narrative power. Some, found chiefly in the bema and western bay of the naos, derive from the Comnenian period (12th century) which is stylistically the finest in Cyprus. They reflect, if obliquely, the glimmer of greatness which the Comnenoi had momentarily retrieved for the Empire, notwithstanding Seljuk, Turkmen and Latin encroachments on the Sea of Marmara. This was a period of profound Constantinopolitan influence on Venice, on Norman Sicily and on the Holy Land. It was during the reign of John II Comnenus that the famous icon, the Virgin of Vladimir, was taken to Kiev, where it bore an inestimable impact on the religious art of Russia.

The finest works at Asinou include a wonderful Dormition of the Virgin (1105) over the west door of the naos – one of the earliest surviving representations of that theme. Christ holds the soul of the infant Mary in His hands while the Apostles strike rhythmical postures of grief and women mourn in the upper galleries. In the north-western recess another fresco portrays, in agonising detail, the maryrdom, at Sebasteia in Armenia Minor, of forty soldiers who died for the Christian faith. Each martyr, bloody and naked, stands on the brink of death in an icy lake. It is interesting that the Christ of the earlier Byzantine imagination personifies more of the hieratic severity of the Hebrews than the human perfections idealised by the Greeks. In later work there emerge humanistic elements more consonant with the anthropomorphism of Hellenic deities such as Apollo. Christ in the later examples is accompanied by a host of angels and the Apostles ride on clouds. At Asinou this characterisation is evident in the paintings executed in other parts of the church during later centuries, especially the fourteenth and fifteenth. The scenes of the Last Judgment (1333), vividly painted on the narthex walls, are as full of recognisable "moderns", with whom we can identify ourselves, as the canvases of Hieronymous Bosch. Wrapped in the coils of spotted serpents and hung over tongues of fire, sinners – among them a Chaucerian gallery: the thief, the gossip, the faithless nun, the dishonest miller – are rewarded in Hell for their earthly misdemeanours. Andreas Stylianou, who is the prime authority on Cypriot

religious painting, suggests that the deceitful miller was probably a caricature of petty despots who managed the water
mills in the adjacent valleys of the Troodos. In any case the
paintings had an explicitly moralising purpose and their
message is not lost on the sceptic of our own day.

The Dumbarton Oaks foundation has cleaned the entire
church and renewed its high-pitched roof. A word of praise
is due to this institution which is formally known as the Center
for Byzantine Studies of Harvard University and is based in
Washington D.C. Once the property of Robert Wood Bliss,
a US diplomat who donated it to scholars, Dumbarton Oaks
incorporates not only a centre for Byzantine studies but
also a museum of pre-Columbian art. The late Mrs. Bliss,
who died in 1969, was like her husband an amateur of both
these cultures, neither of which are generally studied in
Anglo-Saxon countries, and the good work proceeds in Cyprus
at Lagoudhera.

The Church of Panayia tou Arakou at Lagoudhera is not
the easiest of destinations at present, for the shortest route
from Nicosia snakes up the Peristerona Valley to Polystipos
and then becomes a rocky trail better suited to goats and
Land-Rovers than to rented cars. But the views from the final
ascent of the hillside on which Lagoudhera is shelved – and
behind which George Grivas "Dighenis" hid in mountain
caves during the Emergency – are composed of elements,
savage and sylvan, which even individually strike wonder in
the beholder. Like the paddyfields of Yunan, vineyards
clamber up precipitous edges; almond, apple and cherry-trees
sprinkle their seasonal blossom over the terraces that wrinkle
the mountainside; their virginal colours are picked up in the
spartan wash of mountaineer farmhouses.

The church at Lagoudhera (1192) is very simple in plan,
single-aisled, vaulted and, as is customary in the Troodos,
protected by an outer shell of roof and walls three or four
hundred years old. The scaffolding will soon come down to
reveal the full majesty of the 12th century fresco painting

that distinguishes Lagoudhera from most if not all churches
in the Byzantine world, from the Balkans to Trebizond.
The lower skirting of the naos wall is badly spoiled but the
rest of the interior is smothered with frescoes whose stylistic
supremacy is gradually disclosed as the India-rubber plies
laboriously over every inch of surface. The compassionate
Christ Pantocrator, the Evangelists and Archangels of the
dome are among the most celebrated (and less frequently
viewed) instances of Comnenian painting, and there is nothing
insular about Lagoudhera. We may quote Stylianou: "The
classical elegance, the ideal faces imbued with a humanistic
approach, the sculptural draperies with their rhythmic undu-
lations, the fine architectural backgrounds in three dimensions,
the minutely detailed ornaments, the great range and the
harmony of the colours, the uniformity of execution at all
levels, and the symbolic interplay of architecture and decora-
tion, mark these frescoes as a direct product of the neo-
classical School of Constantinople prior to its conquest by the
Crusaders."* It is well that restoration at Lagoudhera has
been entrusted to the expertise of David Winfield and his wife,
an English couple whose services to Byzantium, in Istanbul
and elsewhere, speak for ecumenism and hold out hope for a
belated western interest in the affairs of eastern Christendom.

* A. and J. Stylianou, *Painted Churches of Cyprus*, p. 17.

CHAPTER SIX

Troodos

General description – Troodos hill resorts: winter sport and summer retreats – Trooditissa Monastery – Mount Olympus – The house that Rimbaud built – Makheras Monastery – Solea Valley – Kakopetria – Galatea – Marathasa Valley – Prodhromos – Kalopanayiotis – Kykko Monastery – Paphos Forest

The Olympians of old bequeathed their name to their several residences, not only on the heights of Mount Olympus in Thessaly, but also on lesser peaks of mainland Elis, Laconia and Arcadia and of Euboea and Cyprus. The querulous family of Zeus were, after all, the divinities of all civilised mankind, which is to say of all Greeks, and hence Hellenic man imagined his half-human deities naturally disposed to inhabit earthly places at once visible but inaccessible to the ordinary mortal. Such a dwelling was, and still is, attributed to the Olympus which plots the very centre of Cyprian Troodos. This mountain range, in geology fractured by volcanic turbulence and by the rapid cooling of molten matter upheaved from beneath the sea, is topographically a lofty pyramid rising to its apex at seven thousand feet, in Mount Olympus. Nowadays the gods of ancient Cyprus, Zeus and Aphrodite among them, share their summit with the modern mysteries of an early warning radar system, for the RAF, guardian of a less fabulous ionosphere, maintains its own white domed sanctuary just above the timber line. From most parts of the island, Mount Olympus appears as a delusively close and palpable prospect. Across boundless seas of ripening cereals and thistle-covered tablelands, it represents a cooling deliverance from summer ardours. Clustered around its deified mountain-top are village resorts whose evergreens, crystal climate, constant springs of water, wood cabins and outdoor cafés make an appealing gesture, part aesthetic, part physical. In the Olympian shadow the hill station of Troodos at 5500 feet is coolest, but Prodhromos (at 4600 feet), Platres (3700), Pedhoulas (3600), Moutoullas (2500), Kalopanayiotis (2400), and Kakopetria (2300) are likewise tonic. From January to March, the same places are embedded in deep snow, crisp and dry, and with their centrally-heated hotels, motorised lifts and long unhindered runs, provide skiing in the best of both worlds. The Cyprus Ski Club, with its base at Nicosia but also positioned at the resorts, is bent on magnetising the snow-starved of the Near East. In this sun-soaked island, snow-skiing and skin-diving are, or at least can be, all in a winter's day.

Largest and southernmost of the resorts is Platres, or rather Pano Platres, surrounded by dense pine forests and steep valleys clad in a luxuriance of bracken-fern and bright flora. The country people in unexplored reaches still sprinkle rose water over the stranger's hands and bring out *glika*, preserves of grapes and other sweets for his refreshment. The nightingales of Platres were immortalised by George Seferis and the creative arts are actively indulged there in August, when a Festival takes place. Then the whole of Cyprus brings its crafts to the modern village; Miss Platres is chosen from among the dryads and music is made. Cypriot music is rooted in the ancient modes and tonal systems of the Helladic experience; it was also susceptible to the influences of the Byzantine liturgy and oriental genres. Thus traits of an Achaean past have survived in songs for sowing, harvesting, wine pressing and other folk activities, while a cycle of "klephtic" songs, so-called for the *klephtes* or Greek guerrilla bands who refused to bow to the Ottoman Sultan, may refer to incidental dramas like the abduction of maidens for the Sultan's harem or, in a cycle called the "Bishops", the blood-bath of 1821. Some Cyprian dances were already old in classical times. The sequence of the knife or the scythe, for instance, may well be a survival of the famous Pyrrhic war dance, called *prylis* in Cyprus. Others actually originated in Crete, Asia Minor and the Balkans but became subsumed in the Cypriot idiom. Still others, of the juke-box or *taverna* genus, are variations on the *hassapiko,* that marvellous mode invested with a new coat by Theodorakis, Hadjidakis and other contemporary students of Greek musical tradition. The lute, the fiddle and of course bouzouki are the commonest instruments of the Cypriot ensemble but the electric organ has made a dubious entry. Probably the sheerest nostalgia emanates from the cane flute which once accompanied Pan in Arcady, the *aulos* which still accompanies the shepherd in lonely places. It celebrates the beauty of eternal spring and laments three millenia of man's lost innocence.

Near Platres stands, at an imperious altitude of five thousand feet, the Monastery of Troodhitissa. Baker described it in 1879 as "without any architectural pretensions; it looked like a family of English barns that had been crossed with a Swiss chalet" and himself set to work on its resuscitation :

> We began by cleaning, and I should like to have engaged Hercules, at the maximum of agricultural wages, to have cleaned the long line of mule stables, a dignified employment for which the hero-god was famous; the Augean were a joke to them. The narrow path by which we had arrived was a mere dung-heap, from which noxious weeds, of Brobdignagian proportions, issued in such dense masses that a meeting of British farmers would have been completely hidden by their great enemy.

Though a religious function and unexceptionable cleanliness have been restored to Troodhitissa, its majestic situation over the western edges of the Troodos and the astonishing story of its birth are superior to its architecture. The monastery was from the first associated with an effigy of the Virgin originally encountered in a nearby cave. A shepherd who had lost his goats at night was surprised at the appearance of a glow among the higher rocks and with reverence related his discovery to his fellows. For some time the puzzling light was observed nightly but no one dared investigate it till a priest was called to lead an expedition to the source of this glimmering wonder. The little party at last arrived at a cave in which a lamp burned before a small effigy of the Mother of God, suspended against the wall. But no human trace was to be seen. Close to the cave a monastery was soon built, in the year 990, to enshrine the awesome effigy, and pilgrims from afar set out on the stony journey to the heart of the Troodos. One day a barren but bountiful woman of Beirut came, made a handsome donation and pressed her mouth once to the effigy within the convent and once to the rock entrance of the cave. Several months afterwards this zealous Levantine was rewarded with a son and Conception was added to Apparition as an object of pilgrimage. The son, by the way, was claimed by the monks as their lawful prize and passed his entire life serving the Lady of Troodos.

On the higher flanks of Mount Olympus, capped by the red lights and white caracol of the radar installation, Troodos village is now reached by a wide looping roadway, from which glimpses of the violet rim of sea-coast are caught, between clumps of black pines. It was the British who "discovered" Troodos and turned it into a hill station where idleness and recreation could be pursued without worldly distraction. They called a neighbouring stream Caledonian Falls (still a pleasant place for rambling) and Royal Engineer Captain Kitchener first posted a Union Jack on Mount Olympus. Where the road zig-zags downhill towards Platres, a stern grey edifice peers from the forest. Its Cairngorm style of construction is not inappropriate to pinewoods and it certainly must have given the British Governors of Cyprus, who used it as a summer retreat, a comfortable sense of being at home. But Government Cottage, as it was known, was in part the work of a most unlikely servant of alien rule, the poet Arthur Rimbaud. The French symbolist dedicated no more than four years of his short life to poetry. At seventeen he wrote *le bateau ivre* and at nineteen retired from writing to indulge a compulsive passion for exotic travel. Thus in 1881 he found himself foreman of a French quarry and, at a time when the *tricouleur* was not the most popular of flags on British soil, was commissioned to fashion, at Troodos, this austere symbol of an expanding Raj. In 1883 Rimbaud arrived in Ethiopia where, as a self-styled chieftain, he mastered the vernacular, kept a polyglot harem and disappeared for a time. Presuming him dead, his friend Verlaine published Rimbaud's *Illuminations* (which met with instant acclaim) and the "dead" poet returned to France, heir to handsome royalties. Rimbaud might today be manning a student barricade or hitting the hippy trail to Katmandu. But he was, in 1948, posthumously adopted by a British administration which, perhaps moved by a revived Francophilia, raised at Troodos the following plaque to the memory of an errant Frenchman :

ARTHUR RIMBAUD

POETE ET GENIE FRANCAIS

AU MEPRIS DE SA RE

NOMMEE CONTRIBUA DE

SES PROPRES MAINS A LA

CONSTRUCTION DE CETTE

MAISON MDCCCIXXXI

The south-eastern region of the Troodos Massif is called Pitsilia. It is seldom visited although well populated. Its villages, Khandria, Agros and Palekhori, among them, nest on hillsides terraced with the cultivation of vines, apples and cherries. The bleak whiteness of the houses, their red roofs framed by a bright green vegetation and the dusky outline of the forest, make a strong impression on the eye. From the spurs of the Pitsilian Troodos, Nicosia and the Kyrenia Mountains are plainly visible, while Limassol spreads along the southern coast, a glittering Lilliput. At higher elevations the summer air is so cool that plants akin to heather and hyacinth fleck the wayside, while two or three thousand feet beneath, the *commanderia* villages of the southern slopes, Zoopiyi, Kalokhorio and Ayios Konstantinos, grow the vines of ancient repute, now mainly for overseas shipment.

Makheras Monastery, hidden in the remotest of the eastern hills, has claims to ownership of an icon of the Virgin painted by St Luke in Asia Minor. In the Frankish period, Queen Alice, wife of Hugh IV and an upholder of the Latin rite, was so curious to see this relic that she broke the "men only" rule and was struck dumb in consequence, a condition rectified three years later by a testimony forced from her to the effect that a fragment of the True Cross of Christ, brought to Cyprus by St Helena, was indisputably authentic. If the idea, propagated by Geoffrey of Monmouth in the 12th century, of St Helena's British origin is refuted by eastern Christians, the legend of her discovery of the Cross at Golgotha is so ingrained as to render doubt meaningless. Makheras also remembers two of its former monks who died at Turkish hands. One was Archbishop Kyprianos, hanged in 1821, and the other Yannikios, impaled in 1832 for alleged sedition. Moreover the ravine of the nascent River Pedhieos which flows at the foot of the monastery is redolent of tragedy. For here in 1957 Gregory Afxentiou, second to George Grivas in the EOKA hierarchy, met death in his hide-out, and the track that follows the stream now bears his name. Some of his charred possessions fill a showcase at the monastery.

From Makheras to Nicosia the lonely road, patterned by the shadow of pines and fragrant with their foliage, climbs downhill towards the plain. At the village of Politiko ancient Tamassus was located; of its once great glory only two royal tombs (7th century B.C.) have survived. Its earliest copper workings are dated from 2500 B.C. but the first settlement is attributed to one Thrakofryghes, in the year 4000. As an early *polis*, Tamassus contained shrines to Apollo, Asklepios, Dionysus and Artemis, and Aphrodite in particular was venerated because the three apples which she presented to Hippomenes supposedly ripened on the banks of the Pedhieos. In the 6th century B.C. Phoenicians settled at Tamassus, and in the time of Christ, when Herod the Great had taken lease of Cyprus, a sizeable Jewish population was introduced by the Romans to work the copper. It was to this Jewish community that Paul and Barnabas, guided there by Heraclides, whom they ordained as Bishop of Tamassus, specially ministered. Heraclides, who lived and preached in a cave, was finally beheaded and burned by outraged Greeks, but not before he had converted a good number of citizens and performed all manner of miracles. In death too his wondrous intercessions were no less remarkable. For example a young resident of Nicosia called Yannis was seized with a devil for most of the year 1769. His troubled parents resolved to take him to the shrine of Heraclides on the saint's own day, whereupon the child was "moved to vomit and cast forth from his mouth a snake a span long and two crabs, and he was healed from that hour". For about a century these monsters were preserved, in their regurgitated condition, in the eaves of the little church of the Monastery of St Heraclides, where the skull and a hand bone of the saint are even now lovingly exhibited. If little substance of Tamassus remains, the four hamlets of the area signify the peculiarities of its later citizens. Politiko refers to the politicians, Argates to the labourers, Episkopio to the bishops and Pera means, quite simply, "over the river".

From Troodos two main roads feel their way north across the wrinkled hills till they drop to the valleys of the Solea and Marathasa. The more easterly of these narrowly avoids the asbestos mines of Amiandos and bends through thick forests of fir and plane. It is a busy thoroughfare as town-dwellers take to the hills for long weekends, but the road is very broad and smoothly surfaced. The two big villages of the descent, Kakopetria and Galata, are loved for their orchards and silver poplars, for the living vignette of arched houses and palisaded ravines and the psychological balm of their perennial streams. But they are best distinguished by the sheer scale of their church frescoes, unparalleled in the rest of Cyprus.

At Kakopetria the Church of Ayios Nikolaos tis Steyis ("St Nicholas of the Roof"), whose steep roof and outer shell of protective masonry totally obscure the original domed structure, preserves interior painting from as early as the Macedonian period of Byzantine history. Its most interesting frescoes are indeed its oldest ones (11th century), notably the Raising of Lazarus and the Entry into Jerusalem. These bear strong affinities with contemporaneous churches of Macedonia proper, at Ohrid and Salonika, and remind us that pre-Lusignan Cyprus was in the van of Byzantine experimentation with form. A most unusual Apotheosis of the Sea (12th century) showing a half-naked nereid seated on a fish with arms, and a Resurrection scene (13th century) – strongly suggestive of the classical Descent into Hades – are patent proof that pre-Christian concepts were so alive in eastern Christianity that the old world rediscovered by such western eclectics as Stuart and Revett and the indefatigable Winckelmann seems in retrospect to have been no more than half-submerged under the rubble of barbarian invasion and the weight of an exclusive monotheism. Of 14th century provenance at St Nicholas of the Roof, a Virgin suckling the Child and a shepherd playing a bagpipe are obvious marks of a peasant naïvety which succeeded the more official styles of the Macedonian and Comnenian periods. The small Church of Panayia Theotokos situated at the entrance to the village goes chronologically further and displays many of the more humanised forms of the later frescoes already observed at Asinou.

In the village of Galata a stone's throw below Kakopetria three more churches illustrate the development of Byzantine art after the demise of the Byzantine state. They are all creations of the 16th century, which of course is late by the standards of Lagoudhera or St Nicholas of the Roof, but as stylistic entities, entirely representative of their Italo-Byzantine age, they are very convincing. The Church of Ayios Sozomenos standing on its hillside behind Galata has a complete series of wall paintings done by Symeon Afxentis, whose signature also appears in the small Chapel of the Archangel below. Finished in 1513 this church, dedicated to St Sozomenos, was impaired, but not irrevocably so, by an old mill once established in its yard, and unbecoming graffiti disfigure some of the prelates who adorn the bema but there are, on its upper wall, fine pictorial sequences showing the martyrdom of St George and the life of the Virgin Mary. Individual saints are depicted on the lower walls and the four female martyrs (Saints Paraskevi, Kyriaki, Barbara and Catherine) and St Mamas of Morphou are exceedingly striking.

Galata's tiny Chapel of Panayia Arkhangelos was endowed by the Zacharia family and finished in 1514. All the interior walls of this splendid opus are covered in paintings which have, over four and a half centuries, kept their colours. The figures here presented by the percipient Symeon Afxentis are a veritable gallery of contemporary faces and sartorial fashion. On the upper frieze the story of Christ is re-enacted, and a Nativity scene shows us a bald shepherd in a sheepskin, humouring Joseph in a familiar and endearing manner. Over the north door the Zacharia donors are themselves portrayed, again in revealing detail. Thus Magdalena Zacharia was evidently of Lusignan or Venetian parentage, for she holds a rosary. The Archangel Chapel is now used but once a year, on the 6th September, the Day of the Archangel Michael.

The largest church at Galata, that of Panayia Podithou, was according to an inscription built in 1502 "at the expense and great desire of Lord Monsignore Demetri di Coro and his wife Elena" whose decorative taste was clearly in keeping with the times, for Italianate influences are obvious in both style and thematic treatment. As is customary, the donor, di Coro, seen here as an old man, offers a model of the church to the Virgin. In the apse, a magnificent portrayal of the Last Supper incorporates both a westernised, bearded Judas (he is usually beardless in Byzantine representation) and the figure of Paul who, for reasons not supported by biblical chronology, habitually appears in eastern paintings as an honorary Apostle. The indigo pigment used in the frescoes of the apse to separate the calligraphic frieze has the intensity of blueness seen at St Sophia in Istanbul. The depiction of the Annunciation brings to mind the handling of the same subject by della Francesca. Acoustic jars punctuate the naos walls and the entire church is, like most churches in the Troodos, blanketed by an enormous roof. Podithou Church once formed the central feature of a monastery which, together with many other shrines of the mountains, was visited by the Kievan monk, Vassily Varsky, in 1735. At Galata the Russian noted, with unconcealed ardour, a large Greek populace and absence of Turkish settlers, a wealth of priests, of orchards and running water. All this is true of today, save the observation about priests. Nowadays only one priest, the Rev. Koulentis, is in charge of all the Galata churches and his work is tempered by an agreeable form of leisure. If an Anglican vicar will tend his roses or umpire village cricket, his Orthodox counterpart is as likely to pass a discursive afternoon in the local *kafeneion* or a reflective one at his easel where, in oils, he recreates icons from faded models, in the idiom of today. The priest at Galata portrays more of local landscapes than would have interested earlier iconographers – except perhaps Symeon Afxentis. And in Afxentis he finds a good precedent.

The Solea is just one of the beautiful valleys of the Troodos where Cypriot Christendom has, since the days of Paul and Barnabas, found a sanctuary. The Troodos have, in an island with one hundred and ten saints of its own, more associations with saintly histories than any other part of Cyprus. Of saints revered by all Orthodoxy, George and Marina are perhaps the most popular in Cyprus, at least if we judge by the number of villages named Ayios Yeoryios and Ayia Marina. The Cypriot George is traditionally a hero of the new or full moon and thus specially empowered to cure lunacy, while Marina is credited with an antidote to insomnia. She should be adopted by all those living in the jet age. Religious festivals have, in the remoter Troodos, survived into our own day, quite untarnished by television or mass travel. On New Year's Eve the peasants prepare a plate of *kollipha* (boiled wheat) on which they place a *vasilopita* or cake honouring St Basil of Caesarea, who is patron of New Year's Day. This is made of creamed wheat and is decorated with sesame seeds. A silver coin is kneaded in the cake and whoever finds it is the luckiest member of the family. A morsel of cake and wheat are then taken into a granary, accompanied by a glass of good wine and a lighted candle so that St Basil, who is said to visit every house on the same evening, may have his fill and bless the farmer's grain. On New Year's Day the peasant tries to sneeze, for every sneeze represents a subsequent year of life and prosperity.

At Epiphany, *lokoumadhes* (honey doughnuts) made by the country housewife are offered to evil spirits known as the *kalikantzaroi,* who since All Souls' Day have roamed the fields in the guise of huge balls of cotton. Once samples of the confection have been left on the roof of the house and the spirits propitiated, the village priest may visit on this day, sprinkling holy water. Above all, Easter customs have to do with simple giving and fasting. During Lent the pious peasant, who has already celebrated Ash Wednesday with a picnic of bread and olives, will fast; then on Palm Sunday olive-trees are taken in procession to church. During Holy Week itself the traditional diet is composed of lentils and beans. A re-enactment of the Crucifixion, using wooden images, is staged on Easter Thursday while on Good Friday an image of the dead Christ is lain to rest in the *epitaphion* or shroud which is carried ceremonially about the village. On the Saturday the

A Troodos hill village: Pedhoulas

Stavros tis Psokas in the Paphos Forest

peasant woman bakes *tiropites* (cheese pies); while they are cooking, she may lift a child up high, enunciating meantime her wish that "As I raise this boy may my pies rise too". Before the emblem-laden Easter Sunday services, when black veils are lifted from the iconostasis, an effigy of Judas is hanged from the wall. Young and old stone it and hurl it into a bonfire, expressly prepared in the churchyard. Bonfires were also once built on St John's Day, the 18th July, when peasants roasted green carobs, or "St John's bread" as they were called. While roasting, the beans would jump through the flames, an exercise said to eliminate fleas. Harvest Day or *Protoleia* is universally celebrated in Cyprus on the 6th August, when the first grapes of the year are blessed by the priest. Certain days of every week are suspect to older peasants. Tuesday, because Constantinople fell to the Turks on a Tuesday, and Friday because on that day Christ died on the Cross.

Parallel with the Solea runs the Marathasa valley, approached from Troodos hill station by way of the village resorts of Prodhromos, Pedhoulas and Moutoullas, each surrounded by mixed forest and orchards. At Prodhromos the Cyprus Forestry Training College is situated, and several hotels are set among the trees. The roofs of some houses in the lower settlements belong to a Corrugated Iron Age, still quiet fashionable, as the plastic flower epoch even now dictates domestic taste in some western households. At Kalopanayiotis, where the village street clings to a cliff-edge above a tumbling brook, and where men play tric-trac through the afternoon, another superb monastery stands, at the foot of the gorge. It is seldom visited by strangers, and to enter it one may have to engage a villager to shout one hundred feet down into the chasm where the priest's daughter has access to a key. This is the Monastery of St John Lampadistes, which though disused as a convent, is still a remarkable ensemble of churches, again ornamented with a complete range of fresco painting.

The largest church at Kalopanayiotis, named for St John

Lampadistes, is wedged in the middle of the monastery which commemorates him, and though rebuilt in the 18th century, it continues to hold, in a silver casket pierced by an aperture for devotional lips, the skull of John Lampadistes who was probably born in the 12th century at nearby Lampas, was rendered blind by a magician called upon by the parents of the fiancée he jilted and died at the mature age of 22. There are 15th and 16th century wall paintings narrating the usual biblical episodes, and the priest's daughter was amazed when the author readily recognised certain themes from among them. Possibly she had heard about the British soldiers who practised their firing in the refectory at Bellapais and had concluded, not without a certain logic, that western Christianity was dead or else had never touched upon the education of the English. Epileptics and other invalids still revere the local St John who, like Heraclides before him, was credited with curative powers, and wax facsimiles of afflicted faces and limbs dangle from the church's vaults, awaiting saintly intercession. There is also a 15th century Latin chapel characterised by Italianate wall painting and with two wooden doors beautifully carved in a geometric pattern. But the entire complex resembles a rambling farmhouse; chickens cluck in the grass and, while the girl relates the histories of the separate parts, the women of Kalopanayiotis scrub clothes in the river and a donkey goes through the painful spasms of a sneezing fit.

To the most illustrious of Cypriot monasteries, at Kykko, two narrow but highly spectacular roads lead off from Pedhoulas and Kalopanayiotis respectively. The first bounds over crests and wooden bridges of almost Alpine proportions. The other climbs past the village of Yerakies and mounts a saddle from which much of western Cyprus spreads out in widening ripples to the sea. In spring the whole verge shouts with the vivid and myriad shades of wild flowers: the sensuous cusps of the magenta-hued corydalis, the purple fragility of the Anatolian orchid, the vying brilliance of the violet butterwort. These slopes are dignified by a total absence of humankind; they are peopled, rather, by silent cedars and the ubiquitous Aleppo pine. Then, far cross a valley and poised beneath a forested mountain peak of more than 4000 feet in height, the white towers of Kykko pinpoint the only human island in this verdant ocean. The hilly approaches are now amenable by an exceptionally broad track which has been slashed from the red earth.

At Kykko there is preserved a famous icon of the Virgin (one of three painted by St Luke) which the monastery's 12th century founder, the eremetical Isaias, is supposed to have brought from Constantinople. The church has four times been gutted by fire – the present structures date from 1813 – but the miraculous icon is believed to be intact. Covered by a cloth and not beheld by human eye in four centuries, one can but guess at its aesthetic value and, indeed, wonder whether there is anything there at all. Near the icon, a black hand is meant as an object lesson in restraining one's natural curiosity, for it is said that it represents the paralysed limb of a negro who was bold enough to have lit his pipe on the vigil light. The icon's principal attribute is to compel rain. In times of drought it is removed from its usual setting and turned facing the direction whence relief is expected, usually towards big clouds.

Due to its relative newness, the architecture itself is without historic importance, but everything about it bespeaks untold riches, from the vast iconostasis and the throne of Archbishop Makarios III (similar to that in St John's at Nicosia) to the four ornate chandeliers which gleam in the naos. Two of these come from 19th century Russia for, till 1917, Kykko possessed great latifundia in Caucasia, each of which yielded a considerable wealth. This as a rule materialised in the shape of gospels, icons and the candelabra we have mentioned. Kykko is still a major landowner in Cyprus; entire commercial zones of Nicosia belong to it.

Westwards the evergreens hold sway again. Beneath the

crest of Tripylos (4619 feet) and ten miles from Kykko, a virginal stretch of cedars known as Cedar Valley is protected from the ravages of felling and animal grazing. The great trees here greatly exceed in number their more famous cousins of the Lebanon, and their tall splendour is enhanced by the rivulets which moisten the forest floor. They form but a big grove in the Paphos Forest of the western Troodos, a zone watered by a more generous rainfall than is visited on more easterly mountains. Law conserves the forest animals, and the Cyprus moufflon (the mountain sheep of the Troodos), once hunted to the point of extinction, is an obvious beneficiary. Domestic beasts are less welcome and in particular the goat, which under man's indifferent eye once practically devastated the island's primeval woods, is forbidden entry to the forest. It is little wonder how unfavourably the Bible compares this creature to the less rapacious sheep. Goats are still plentiful in lowland areas; indeed they are as necessary to rural Cyprus as the camel to Arabia, and in former times, when timber was less valuable, they were a political issue. Goats meant votes. Man was an even older offender. Phoenicians and Romans hewed trees for the tunnels of copper mines. Alexander the Great and the Venetians used Cyprian wood for their fleets and by the time of the Ottomans, lumber proved so scarce that it had to be floated across the strait from Anatolia.

Today much of Cyprus is again timbered. In the Troodos the Aleppo pine (*pinus halepensis*) flourishes everywhere except above a height of 4000 feet on Mount Olympus, where the black pine (*pinus negra*) takes over. The cones of the latter yield small edible nuts picked by the country people. Plane trees (*platanus orientalis*) grace every river dale where also grow the wild almond, alder, maple, myrtle, ilex and tere-binth. The roads of the sparse Mesaoria are often adorned by eucalyptus and acacia, while the village landscape encompasses groves of olive and carob. Of the crops cultivated in the plain, wheat and barley are commonest. Ripening as early as April and May they are customarily grown on a one-year fallow system. The wilder coastal reaches of Cyprus, particularly the Akamas and Karpas, are often a tangled scrub of juniper, oleander and lentisk, natural custodians of small fauna, and, as we have seen, the north coast is enriched by orange and lemon plantations. Though not native, palms thrive in the lush surrounds of Lefka and Larnaca. As for the cypress, it too is an emotive ornamentation thoroughly acclimatised on Cypriot soil. Sacred to Hercules, who himself planted the famous grove at Daphne outside Athens, the cypress cult was Minoan in origin and may have been directly introduced from Crete.

At Stavros tis Psokas, in a glade of the north-western Paphos Forest, the Forestry Department runs a Rest House where, for a small fee, the traveller can esconce himself in a woodland idyll, explore the forest, climb the pine bluffs of the western hills and gaze out at the half-moon of Khrysokhou Bay or at the ancient walls of Kykko tucked under its Arcadian knoll. The Cypriots were clever to hide so many of their monasteries in such seclusion. Small wonder that Kykko, Troodhitissa and Makheras have provided political as well as spiritual asylum in their lengthy history, to EOKA partisans as well as theologians.

CHAPTER SEVEN

Paphos

*Petra tou Romiou: the birthplace of Venus – Palaia Paphos –
Yeroskipos – Nea Paphos and Ktima: monuments and
museums – Coral Bay – St Neophytus Monastery – Cypriot
icons – Khrysorroyiatissa Monastery – Polis – Fontana
Amorosa and the Akamas Peninsula*

Few who have seen it have not fallen in love with the country
of Paphos. For, in relative isolation and peace, it is a dis-
tillation of the essential Cyprus. Crossing its quiet sugar fields,
the motorist has the pleasant sensation of arriving at the end
of the way. It is like reaching Kalamata in the southern
Peloponnese, for agriculture and the sea are the determinants
of its character, together with a nostalgic pride in ancient
glories. A large empty road approaches it by the southern
shore, sometimes raised on the table-top of cliffs running perpendicular to the sea, sometimes swooping smoothly to the
water's edge, between blinding walls of chalk on one side and
a fringe of aromatic shrubbery on the other. Of a sudden a
craggy prominence appears. This is a landing stage of the
deities, called variously Petra tou Romiou and Aphrodite's
Rock. Where the waves unfurl themselves with most vigour is
where Aphrodite, doubtless aided by the zealous sea-zephyr,
delivered herself from the churning foam. Nature still calls
forth the Goddess. Idleness is productive, for the place at once
evokes a mystical communion. Tempted by the dazzling land,

a greenish sea caresses it, only to recede time and time again. Polychrome pebbles make up the beach and not a sole human installation mars the primal spot where the Goddess of Greek Amours made her frothy début. Masters of euphemism, the travel pamphleteers avoid the oldest Hellenic theories about her divine conception. In fact she is quite simply a union of salt and phallus, for the genitalia of Uranus – brutally severed by his vengeful son Cronus – had lately impregnated the Aegean. Most lovers of myth will agree to the famous undress in which she disembarked. And perhaps also to that peculiar form of propulsion which Botticelli gave her, a scallop shell. The guide book recommends a "sentimental stop" at this point and, sure enough, three English matrons emerge from their car to have a look, applying lipstick as if fearing competition.

So much for the more romantic tale. We learn from Herodotus that Palaia Paphos (Old Paphos), whose site is further west, was founded by Phoenician colonists from Askalon, who brought with them both Astarte and Tammuz, later hellenised, as we have seen, as Aphrodite and Adonis. With today's vulgarisation of Venus, it is surprising to learn that for the Phoenicians of Byblos and Palaia Paphos her pristine image was a white cone or pyramid and that her sanctuary provided a milieu for ritual harlotry in which, as Sir James Frazer notes in the *Golden Bough,* "the practice was clearly regarded, not as an orgy of lust, but as a solemn religious duty performed in the service of that great Mother Goddess of Western Asia". The pecuniary proceeds from ceremonial love were dedicated to Astarte and it was not till her hellenisation that, from the 8th century onwards, she was transformed into the bathing beauty of the *aphros* and not till Alexandrian times that the supply of *ierodouloi* or temple-maidens actually exceeded demand, hence lending Cyprus the now little advertised distinction of being the first country to nationalise its strumpets. Virgil says that in his day the Goddess had not only a famous temple at Paphos but also one hundred altars and a huge priesthood which must have worked overtime during the festivals of *Aphrodisia* in spring, and *Adonia,* held at Amathus in summer. Her cult spread all through Magna Graecia, especially to Cythera and Cnidus, and to Cape Eryx in Sicily. According to some, she was, by Anchises, the mother of Aeneas. Not for many centuries did the more wanton aspects of the Aphrodite cult make room for reason. As late as 1528 the Paduan geographer Benedetto Bordone, part bemused and part disdainful, was unable to omit from his brief description of Cyprus the remark that "the first woman who made a habit of selling her body for money was in this island".

As for Palaia Paphos several stories were advanced to explain its beginnings. In the *Metamorphoses* (*X*), Ovid attributes the city's foundations to the son of Pygmalion and the animate Galatea, whose name was 'Paphos'. *Illa Paphum genuit, de quo tenet insula nomen.* But the more usual is to ascribe them to its first king, Cinyras, sometimes called the father of Adonis. A Paphos certainly existed in the Homeric age for the *Odyssey* (*VIII*) relates the steps leading "laughter-loving Aphrodite to Paphos, where she has her sacred precinct, and an altar fragrant with incense". Near the village of Kouklia part of the temple of Aphrodite is just discernible, thanks to the British Museum excavations of 1888, but a combination of reading and imagination will help re-create the lustre of Ovid's "navel of the world" as it existed before the destructive earthquakes of A.D. 332 and 342 and the decree of Emperor Theodosius putting an end to the mysteries, games and feasts of the pagans.

On the highway to Paphos in the direction of the setting sun, the pagan pilgrims would stop at Yeroskipos (Holy Garden). Today's village of that name possesses, like Peristerona, a five-domed Byzantine church, which is dedicated to St Paraskevi. Three axial domes and two squat cupolas are set above the transepts. The villagers make Turkish delight. Ten miles west of Kouklia or ancient (Palaia) Paphos, we find the modern town of Ktima, perched above its port which is referred to as Nea (New) Paphos, or as Kato (Lower) Paphos. Indeed Ktima itself is often simply "Paphos", however inaccurate that may seem to scholars. Nea Paphos has harboured ships since Palaia Paphos attracted Venus-worship and it is today a major archaeological zone. Tradition informs us that Agapenor of Trojan celebrity, son of Ancaeus and grandson of Lycurgus, was driven on this shore by a tempest and founded Nea Paphos, to which he then led a colony of fellow Arcadians. If that fact appears doubtful, it is certain that this coastal city was the creation of merchants serving the neighbouring settlement of Palaia Paphos. But while in Hellenistic and Roman times the latter sank into insignificance, the former port remained populous and, damaged by tremors in the reign of Augustus, was restored by him and named, in the year 15 B.C., Augusta. Cicero governed here when it constituted the island's capital under Rome, and his successor Sergius Paulus was the first official of the Empire to be converted to the Christian faith, by Paul and Barnabas, whose visit to Paphos (c. 45) is reported in the New Testament:

And when they had gone through the isle unto Paphos, they found a certain sorcerer, a false prophet, a Jew whose name was Barjesus

Which was with the deputy of the country, Sergius Paulus, a prudent man; who called for Barnabas and Saul, and desired to hear the word of God.

But Elymas the sorcerer withstood them, seeking to turn away the deputy from the faith.

Then Saul (who is also called Paul), filled with the Holy Ghost, set his eyes on him,

And said, O full of all subtlety and all mischief, thou child of the devil, wilt thou not cease to pervert the right ways of the Lord?

And now, behold, the hand of the Lord is upon thee, and thou shalt be blind, not seeing the sun for a season.

And immediately there fell on him a mist and a darkness;
and he went about seeking some to lead him by the hand.
Then the deputy, when he saw what was done believed,
being astonished at the doctrine of the Lord. *Acts XIII*

Nea Paphos was sacked and burnt by the Saracens in 648
and suffered at the hands of the Genoese in 1372. Cognisant
of the port's vulnerability and profiting from the fertility of
the Paphiot hinterland, the Frankish Lusignans removed the
centre of the city uphill to their *ktima* or "domain", whence
derive its present name and position.

Ktima or modern Paphos is a sunny town of some ten
thousand souls, the nucleus of a prosperous agriculture. Its
freshness of appearance is due in part to reconstruction after
the earthquake of 1953. Ktima claims no ancient architecture
of its own but has chosen the Doric and Ionic styles for some
of its civic monuments. Its District Museum (in George Grivas
Dighenis Avenue) contains an extensive collection of archaeological discoveries from the whole of western Cyprus, and
above all from Palaia Paphos, Nea Paphos and Marium-
Arsinoe. From the latter comes the island's finest funeral stele,
a fragmented masterpiece of relief carving of the 5th century
B.C. Another sculpture of interest is a marble torso of
Aphrodite, suitably recovered from the sea. There are, too,
objects from the current excavations at Nea Paphos. The
Curator of the Museum, Professor Eliades, also has an absorb-
ing collection of sherds and artefacts which he has excavated
at Nea Paphos and keeps at his house (1 Exo Vrysis Street).
Interested strangers can approach him directly for a special
viewing. A small Byzantine Museum in the Episcopal Palace
and a Turkish Museum, next to the Yeni Jami (New Mosque)
illustrate, chronologically, the later periods of Paphiot history.
The three thousand Turks of the town (which they call *Baf*)
are perceptibly better integrated than in some larger towns
and there is about contemporary Paphos a tangible gentleness
which commends it to the world-weary.

Nea or Kato Paphos is still a haven for small cargo ships loading sugar, tobacco, cotton and fruit, and for the local fishing fleet. Fish, which is so often absent from east Mediterranean menus, is here discharged from caïques for instant consumption in the waterside restaurants. A stocky Turkish fortress guards the shallow anchorage; the Ottomans learned a lot from the West. Paphos Fort, for instance, resembles very closely the Venetian castle at the harbour entrance to Heraklion. Having emerged from their Altaic *Urland,* the Turks proved again and again that adaptability is a key to power. Drawing from the experience of Byzantine Greeks, of Muslim Arabs and the Latin West, and still charged with the simple energy of wanderers, the conquering sons of Osman constructed their imperial edifice from composite parts.

The exciting thing about Nea Paphos is that, though much has already been unearthed, there is still so much more to be done. Throughout most of the Ptolemaic and Roman hegemonies Paphos, like Salamis, formed a prime repository of the Greek Cypriot tradition. It was first to be governed by a *demos* (popular assembly) and a *boule* (council) and in the time of Septimus Severus it received the title *iera metropolis ton kata Kypron poleon* (the sacred metropolis of all Cyprian towns). The *Koinon Kyprion,* which supervised observance of the imperial cult and the minting of coins, was centred at Paphos, thus entrusting to the city a heavy responsibility for transmitting ancestral custom. Zeus and Leto, with their twin offspring Apollo and Artemis, and of course with Aphrodite, were venerated in Paphos.

Since 1961, when fragments from it were struck by a ploughman going about his labour, a Roman villa has attracted probably the broadest publicity of any ancient place in Cyprus. On account of the god's recurrent portraiture in the mosaics of the floor, the villa has been designated the House of Dionysus. Its original walls vanished with earth tremors, but the floors of various rooms, of the atrium and tablinum above all, remain to give us a magnificent series of late 3rd century mosaics, second to none in countries ruled from Rome. Classical myths are narrated in proto-technicolor. Pyramus and Thisbe, Dionysus and Icarus, Apollo and Daphne, Hippolytus and Phaedra enact their fateful parts on a vivid stage of geometric patterns and leaping beasts. In the tablinum creatures of the woodland romp among trees and vines. A band of rinceaux runs around them. Strong black lettering spells out, in Greek, the larger tableaux. A metal canopy now protects the mosaics from the brilliance of the sun, but the pale grass and vetch growing at its edges preserve some of that unready element which must have caught the ploughman unawares. Close to the villa and just below the whitewashed lighthouse of Kato Paphos, the outline of a Roman theatre obtrudes from rock and vegetation. An amphitheatre crowns the headland. Beneath it a Byzantine castle, locally called Saranta Kolones (Forty Columns) from the broken pillars which once littered its precincts, is under pick and shovel. In the north-eastern angle of the ancient wall of Nea Paphos another theatre quite unexcavated, and a labyrinth of underground chambers called the Catacomb of Ayia Solomoni, pose further questions as yet unanswered. About the latter all that can be ascertained is a late use, in the 12th century, as a Christian sanctuary, for several frescoes decorate its gloomy walls. Some of these have since been subjected to the idle scribblings of visitors, Crusaders among them.

On the northern perimeter of the original city, the name of Dighenis again denotes a natural phenomenon, the Petra tou Dhiyeni, a giant stone hurled by the Cypriot hero at a local queen who declined his offer of marriage. Dighenis, it seems, was busy at Paphos because Aphrodite's spume-crested rock takes its usual name, Petra tou Romiou, from another of his exploits. On that occasion he scattered a whole Saracen fleet with a mere sprinkling of boulders.

Outside the confines of classical Nea Paphos and towards the western sea, a forgotten terrain of dry grass, scrub and limestone outcrops provides some townspeople with a rubbish dump, and many a reader of the guide-books, directed hither to see three Tombs of the Kings, will have turned away without finding his objective. He should persevere, because once their entrances are perceived the Tombs, which compose a necropolis of the 3rd century B.C., are visitable. Though unlikely to have immured the royal dead, their rock-hewn chambers, framed at the entrance by a Doric façade, exert a morbid fascination. Our ignorance of their history is to be regretted. In its physical scale and historical prestige Nea Paphos was a metropolis of its time. Year by year the diggers, at present Poles and Britons, uncover a little more of its quality.

Not far from Paphos are hill hamlets like Emba and Arodhes where the spirit of the Middle Ages is not extinguished. Few foreigners or even citizens of eastern towns come this far and the motor-car is a rarity. Older peasants will hitch a ride over mountainous roads, offering even the incredulous foreigner a coin as recompense. The country which approaches the horn of western Cyprus is probably the least spoiled of all. If some geological upheaval were suddenly to thrust this coast seven hundred miles towards Italy, its deserted bays would swiftly achieve commercial fame and desecration. The Government has plans for a holiday village near Peyia, and there is already a small reservoir on the Mavrokolymbos River. But such beaches as Coral Bay and others less accessible will hopefully go unmolested for another decade at least. Their pink sands, composed of minute fragments of coral and backed by low cliffs of rock and scrub, still enjoy silence and isolation.

Drive at the end of a day through the olive-groves of the Paphiot hinterland to the Monastery of Ayios Neophytos and ask the monks if you may pass a night in their care. Many monasteries in Cyprus maintain the custom of keeping rooms free for the wayfarer, who expresses his gratitude, if not in prayer, in a donation to the box. Monasticism for the Orthodox enjoins a high degree of devotion to God, but also to the community, and the monk's worldliness determines his good relations with the latter. At supper three generations will be consuming fruits of the monks' labour, a meal which is anything but ascetic. Seated at table are a sage with the dignity of an early prophet, a robust round-faced brother with a ribald humour and a young monk who has many years before him to grow his beard. Whereas brethren would once journey from one monastery to another during a lifetime, a more local commitment is now preferred. In early adolescence the aspirant will take three days off from school to live with the monks. Then, on leaving school, he rejoins the fraternity as a novice, remaining with it for some ten years till proceeding to theological studies undertaken at the universities of Athens or Salonika, or at Mount Athos. Finally, he returns to dedicate the rest of his years to the same monastery. In Cyprus the social and educative rôle of the Church gives the priesthood and monastic body so substantial a prestige that many parents are at least as happy to see their sons in vestments as in pin-stripes or military uniform. The secular and religious life of the island are nothing so divorced from one another as they are in the majority of modern countries.

The site of the monastery again monopolises a gushing spring. Its fecundity supports a thriving agriculture. The orchards below and the fields, furrowed in meander-shapes, are worked by the monks themselves, their produce destined for Paphos market. With more urbanity than their isolation would suggest, the monks imbibe wines, smoke heady tobacco and hoard anecdotes for unsuspecting strangers. Their true devotions are punctuated by the usual services held in the big church: *orthros* in the morning and *esperinos* in the evening. On Sundays the *liturgia* honours a particular saint. In an island whose countless monasteries are bound up with the memory of so many and extraordinary human miracles, St Neophytus occupies a special place, probably because the saint exemplified the simplest of beatitudes. Neophytus was born in the mid-12th century at Lefkara, the present-day lace-making village, and from infancy he desired to become a monk. But at eighteen his parents chose a bride for him and he fled for three months to the Monastery of Ayios Chrysostomos. One legend says that he married the girl and disappeared on the wedding night. After a visit to Jerusalem, Neophytus decided upon an ascetic life and sought forthwith an isolated cliff-face near Paphos. Having scoured from the rock three caves, he set about making them habitable as his own private sanctuary, or *Enkleistra,* far from the madding Middle Ages. One cave he turned into a chapel, to be illumined in 1183 with frescoes painted by Theodorus Afsefthis, a friend. Neophytus dedicated his tiny chapel to the Holy Cross and himself carved its altar. A diminutive bema and vestry were added; an adjoining cave furnished the hermit with an early version of bed-sitter, in which he fashioned, again in stone, a table and a bed, the latter still covered with a hair mattress. After seven years as a recluse, Neophytus was persuaded to allow other holy men to join him, and the monastery thus took root. In later life, at the age of 64 and bothered by the crowds of gaping pilgrims who disturbed his solitude, he excavated another cell for himself higher up the cliff and accessible only by ladder. From this retreat, which he called New Zion, he followed services through a hole in the chapel roof and descended only on Sundays to counsel his disciples. When he died he was laid to rest in a grave dug by his own exertions, but today his relics repose in a wooden sarcophagus kept in the 15th century domed church nearby. A silver reliquary encloses his oft-kissed skull, and pilgrims from as far as Australia come to look at his hand-made memorial. Rarely can any man have shaped so much of his environment. The frescoes of the rock chambers are of varying virtue. Dumbarton Oaks is at work on their restoration; already the overall brightness of their setting belies the notion that caves are for spelæologists.

Neophytus left posterity fifteen works of literature, among them a Ritual Ordinance revered by all Hellenes and a set of homilies whose simple and judicious ethic calls to mind Thomas à Kempis. Some of these are seen in the Bibliothèque Nationale in Paris. For the hermit of Paphos, fear of God and memory of death were keys to the upright life; yet his philosophy lacked neither vigour nor warmth. "Always imitate well the industrious bee which diligently prepares honey and gathers wax," he preached, and "always practise the works of joy". He still holds a cherished place in the hearts of Eastern Christendom as the incarnation of goodness and since rediscovery in 1750 of the saint's body which "yet retained its skin and diffused a sweet smell", a pious train has trundled up the small valley to his shrine. During the 19th century the monastery was guardian of a creed both theological and national and in 1821, when clerics took the brunt of Ottoman persecution, the Abbot Melissovouccas refused the insidious invitation of Kuchuk Mehmet to come to Nicosia, and instead remained at the *Enkleistra*. A military detachment was sent against him and for a while the besieged monks found refuge in the refectory. The Turkish bullet holes scar its doorway to this day. Escaping to the hills, where he was tended by a shepherdess, the Abbot was in the end betrayed, led to Nicosia and, on refusing to abjure his religion, impaled.

The artistic marvel of the main church at the Monastery is perhaps the 16th century icon-painting which forms the Deisis of the iconostasis – individual portraits of Christ, the Virgin, Archangels, Apostles and St Paul, each stooped in a pose of absolute candour. A word about the technique of iconography. As a rule the panel is covered first with canvas and then with a layer of reinforcing gesso, upon which the paint is laid. This is the Byzantine method of preparation, one which originated in the mummy paintings of Egypt. survived through the entirely early Christian era and was adopted by the Orthodox world in the 11th and 12th centuries. The forests of Cyprus afforded the icon-painter hardwood of a resilience scarce enough in Greece or Russia, whose

Making lace at Lefkara

Music-making

Near Fontana Amorosa

The Tekke of Hala Sultan

icon panels tend thus to be severely bent. The presence in
Cypriot icon-painting of certain non-Byzantine colours such
as turquoise suggests a western source for oils; otherwise the
pigments and mixing formula of egg-yolk and glue or mastic
obeyed the conventions of Orthodox painting. Many of the
best icons of Cyprus recently travelled west in an exhibition
of the "Treasures of Cyprus", and the Cypriot Church hopes
to install in Nicosia a museum devoted to the uncelebrated
wonders of its Byzantine art.

Across the nearest spur of hills and the oak-clad village of
Kili, the road labours mightily towards Polis. This ridge is in
fact a seismic fault, and the big village of Stroumbi unhappily
found itself at the very epicentre of the 1953 earthquake. Its
new prefabrications are as anonymous – and 'quake-resistant
– as modern Agadir or Skoplje, but to complain would be to
miss the point, for the casualties in 1953 were high. Although
a Cypriot adage has it that if many dogs bark in the evening
there will come an earthquake, village dogs like nothing better
than to howl at a summer's moon – and tremors have been
almost as rare as comets. Stroumbi gets its name from a fat
man (*stroumbes*) who in Comnenian days was a lord of the
district. Today it is the bulging countryside, and above all the
vineyards which bespeak fatness. A branch road turns inland
to gather up a season's harvest and to explore the wooded
highlands where priests have sought their solace and vocation.
Indeed, Pano Panayia is the birthplace of President Makarios,
whose early life followed a characteristically Cypriot course,
first as novice at Kykko, then as an outstanding scholar at
the Pancyprian Gymnasium. On the steep edge, in a situation
of ineffable grandeur, lies the Monastery of Khrysorroyiatissa,
allegedly named after the "golden breasts" of the Virgin,
whose physical attributes were never quite tabu in an island
which had once adored Venus. Her wondrous icon ascribed,
again, to St Luke is now sheathed in a silver case, but it is
much venerated, particularly by criminals. A facsimile engrav-
ing of the original, made by the Cretan painter Kornaros, is

displayed in the church. This monastery calls for affection more than awe. "I am," says the poet-monk, "a happy mortal for I live in one of the tiny brilliant stars that decorate the firmament of beautiful Paphos. This excellent star, the Monastery of Khrysorroyiatissa, is fixed on the high breast of a great mountain away from its celestial brethren, that it might remind us of their glory."

The ride from Stroumbi down to the Bay of Khrysokhou is a truly pastoral one, opening superb views across several broad and fertile vales to Tripylos, Olympus and other sentinels of the Troodos. The young vines are interspersed with errant poppies. Cumuli floating like balloons cast deep shadows on the dappled hills. Widening to accomodate habitation, the valley of the Stavros Psokas points towards the sea, and constant herds of chestnut-tufted goats with drooping ears and curled tails hinder the traveller, to the chagrin of women, both old and young, who shout gruff commands whenever a car goes by. And so to Polis tis Khrysokhous (City of the Golden Land), or Polis for short, a little town which, since barricades were implanted on the Kokkina coast, represents a sort of terminus for Cypriot traffic, though not for the tourist who should proceed along the splendid bay to Pomos and beyond.

Ironically the large Turkish minority of Polis is so well integrated that bilingualism is still the rule in shop signs. This is a good omen. Total integration is of course neither feasible nor desirable, as this would mean repudiation by one side of its culture, of its language and especially its religion. For religious loyalty is the ultimate distinction. Speaking of some prosperous Nicosia merchant, a Greek may contradict the visitor who is at pains to label each and every nationality: "No, he's no Armenian, he's a Christian!" In the rural areas of Cyprus, church and mosque even more than language or dress mark the two poles of allegiance. It is said that one may tell whether a dog belongs to a Christian or a Muslim by observing the position in which he lies. If he crosses his legs

it means that his owner is a Christian. It is a thousand pities
that politics stress the divergences rather than affinities between Greeks and Turks. These two peoples possess more in
common than they usually admit. The Cypriot Turks are, as
we have seen, to a large extent islamised "Anatolians", heirs
to Alexander and Byzantium as much as Mohamed and the
Osmanlis. The chronology of Graeco-Turkish tension is as old
as the Ottoman conquest of the Hellenic world, more dramatic
but less consistent that the record of peaceable amity which
has also, on a day-to-day basis, characterised their relations.
The catalogue of atrocities committed in the name of race
and religion (Ottoman extermination of the Greeks of Chios
or Constantinople in the Greek War of Independence and at
Smyrna in 1922, or the massacre and mutilation of Morean
Muslims in the same war and the practical annihilation by
Greeks of Cretan Muslims in 1897) show sporadic excesses
of zeal to be the monopoly of neither side. As in Ireland,
re-kindled animosities feed voraciously on the embers of
unforgotten and unforgiven precedents. The Greeks and
Turks of Polis and Paphos must be less haunted by history
than their confrères of Nicosia or Famagusta, where physical
separation has led Turkish radicals to demand absolute partition for their community. As such Polis is a happy place.
And its happiness is enhanced by a profusion of orange trees
and natural gardens.

On a neighbouring mound stood the ancient city of Marium,
whose fragments are now principally in the Paphos Museum.
Marium, a city-kingdom founded in the 7th century by
Athenians, was destroyed in 312 B.C. by Ptolemy I who
accused its king, Stasieikes, of supporting the Syrian king,
Antigonus, in the latter's scheme to occupy the island. A new
city was built by Ptolemy Philadelphus (285–247 B.C.) on
the site of modern Polis and renamed Arsinoe, after Ptolemy's
sister. The city throve under this name during the Roman
and Byzantine periods, but was changed to the present Polis
by the Lusignans.

Further down the Akamas Peninsula an asphalt lane leads from Polis to Lachi, a photogenic hamlet with minuscule harbour for fishing tacks, and continues as far as the natural spring called Fontana Amorosa where the water bubbles from the mountainside between foliage and fronds. The Renaissance poet Ariosto describes it in *Orlando Furioso*: "There is a slope of seven miles in length which rises gradually from the seashore planted with myrtle, cedar, bitter oranges and laurel and many other aromatic trees, bushes, roses, lilies and crocuses, giving off a very beautiful scent, which the sea breeze wafts from the earth and carries into the sea. From a crystal spring a stream has its source and traverses this zone which, with all the enchanted surroundings, are dedicated to Venus." Indeed the fountain is often known as the Baths of Aphrodite. But paradise does not cease at this point, for the ensuing shore has few rivals. With the verdancy of Corfu and Corsica and the sheer panoramas of the Bays of Naples and Mirabello, the Akamas, which is uninhabited, has the extra virtue of complete isolation. No more than a rough track winds towards Cape Arnauti between the fragrant trees and the sea. The stupendous bay veers eastwards to meet the mountains head-on while below the water has carved miniature craters, organ-pipes and natural chairs in the igneous stone. Driftwood collects on the beaches. Thick scrub clambers up the towering tableland where the eagle has its home. Towards evening the sound of one hundred similar bells wings in on the distant air and a motley herd of little goats charges suddenly over a bluff. They are attended by a young herdsman who sings *hassapiko* for all his lungs are worth, interrupting himself to goad the animals with plausible imitations of a bird-call. Nowhere in Cyprus has the Creator lavished such careful detail on the essential landscape, and seascape.

CHAPTER EIGHT

Limassol

Limassol and the Commanderia – Akrotiri Peninsula – Cape Gata – Kolossi Castle – Wine industries – Curium and the Sanctuary of Apollo – Amathus

As an ancient but insignificant village called Nemesos, Limassol was no metropolis until Crusaders discovered its value as a haven, and its wines. Once, by a meteorological accident, Richard Lionheart had married his Berengaria here in the chapel of St George (1191) and had seen her crowned Queen of England by the Bishops of York and Évreux, Limassol was to enjoy two golden centuries. Soon the Hospitaller Knights of St John leased the neighbouring castle of Kolossi from the Lusignans and cultivated the radiant slopes around it. Excepting an interlude following the Fall of Acre (1291), when the Knights Templar took brief residence, the Hospitallers established the Grand Commanderia, a fiefdom of some sixty villages. The Commanderia at Kolossi was the richest of all Hospitaller possessions save Rhodes; its sugar-cane and wine put Cyprus on the maps of European merchants. Then came flood and fire. Most of the city was burned in the 14th century by the Genoese. In the 15th century Mamelukes made it the object of their destructive inroads. An earthquake in 1567 put an end to Venetian attempts at improving the fortress and, in 1570, 70,000 Turkish infantry, 30,000 cavalry and 200 cannon delivered the *coup de grâce,* in effect obliterating the

town. Some 20,000 citizens were butchered and by the early
19th century the population had dwindled to 150 souls. But
after 1878 Great Britain, who wished Limassol to be the
Liverpool of Cyprus, saw to the harbour, imported work and
workers and boosted the town's income, size and prestige.
Limassol (Greek *Lemesos*, Turkish *Lemesun*) is today the
island's second city. That a British population in its environs,
at the Akrotiri base and suburban Episkopi, should have
survived has a nice historic symmetry about it.

For those who seek the past Limassol offers little but the
castle near the harbour. This was the first Cypriot fortification
to fall to Lala Mustafa. It is now occupied by soldiers.
Since the latter have closed it to visitors "till further notice",
the District Museum housed within its walls, the Great Hall
which British administrators used as a gaol till 1940, and
the chapel where Lionheart was wedded will go unvisited.
But Limassol has modernity by way of compensation: the
biggest supermarkets, the liveliest night-clubs and perhaps
the best shopping in Cyprus. Its Miramare Hotel is a
luxurious sun-trap on the bland water's edge, and the outlying countryside, wedged narrowly between mountain and
Mediterranean, is diversified even by Cypriot standards.

Immediately south of Limassol on the Akrotiri, that con-
tourless peninsula with salt lake in winter and salt pans in
summer, two worlds live strangely juxtaposed. There is the
Akrotiri of the Sovereign Base Area where British radio instal-
lations punctuate the prosaic marshes, their spectral antennae
reflected in the brackish pools like pine-trees in Sung water-
colours. Road-signs warn reed-laden donkeys and their peasant
masters to beware of loud and sudden noises from diving jets.
An occasional black face is discernible in the citrus groves
and vineyards of Phassouri, a curious anomaly explained by
the inter-marriage between Cypriot immigrants to Africa with
negro women who later returned to Cyprus with their families.
Fresh pitch and the shade of tall trees darken the highways,
which are heaped with oranges in season.

Apart from the familiar caricature faces of the Royal Air Force, there is also a variegated feathered population, equally migratory. Since the island lies almost due north of the Nile delta – that artery from the very heart of Africa whence myriad birds leave their winter-quarters for Europe and Asia – some three hundred species visit Cyprus, from the Siberian starling and Palestine bulbul to the smew, little stint, dotterel and pin-tailed sandgrouse. The island has over forty resident species moreover, endemic breeds of chaffinch, chat and jack-daw for instance. Most of these are found at some time of year in the Akrotiri, though summer heat and drought often force birds to rear their young in the cooler clime of the hills. Seekers of exotica should come in winter months, for it is then that huge flocks of flamingo (*phoenicopterus ruber roseus pallas*) arrive at the Salt Lake from the Caspian Sea. Over eight thousand have been seen on one day alone, if not with ease, for a flock usually remains far from land, its presence betrayed by its occasional flights and the odd pink feathers on the lake-shore. Young arrivals may reach no higher than their parents' bellies. Each corner of the island is associated with certain species : the Karpas with the eternal June sound of the lark, the uplands with the whirr of the quail and francolin, the mountain redoubts with the eagle, bustard and *gyps fulvus fulvus* or griffon vulture. The latter lays one solitary egg in a cup-like nest some fifteen inches across and constructed from dry grass and palmetto. Beginning with the innards and ending with the flesh, it feeds on dead donkeys and other carrion. In copses of oak, the night-loving *thupi* cries in hollow augury of spring; a folk song warns us that this augury may be false.

At one time the remotest reaches of the Akrotiri were infested with snakes, and the present name of its farthest promontory, Cape Gata, derives from the cats which the monks of Ayios Nikolaos Monastery trained for hunting serpents. These cats were so famous in the Middle Ages that bequests were made to the monastery for their proper upkeep.

Every day, just as sporting dogs pursue game, they would chase the reptiles and kill those they caught. At the clang of a bell they went home and after dinner sallied out again, not returning till late in the evening. Though their appearance is nowadays rare enough, two venomous varieties of snake live in the dry scrub. One is the *kouphi* which, despite its short tabular shape, was observed by the author motionless upon a ledge of the sheer wall at Bellapais Abbey, feigning death and doubtless anticipating a dinner of sparrow or lizard. The other is the *saittaros,* sleek and greyish and swift to regain its hole in the earth at the approach of human feet. Lizards, which love to make their homes in the crannies of ancient and abandoned cities, are far more numerous.

Till a century ago Cyprus suffered almost yearly catastrophe in the locust plagues which "obscured the splendour of the sun". Many literate travellers kept records of this horror. "At once," wrote one such, "they come down like hail from heaven, eat everything voraciously and are driven before the wind in such enormous flights that they appear as dense clouds. They devour every green herb, and dying at last of hunger leave behind them a terrible stench, which infects the air and soil, and breeds a fearful pestilence. The natives seek out their eggs with diligence and destroy their nests". The scourge of 1668 lasted one month and the Pasha ordered all women to bring a certain measure full of the insects to his palace. Then he had holes dug outside the city where they were buried under earth lest "their infection pollute the air". That spurious Arab, Ali Bey el Abbasi – whose real name was Don Domingo Badia-y-Leyblich – actually wrote a memorandum on the subject to the Archbishop of Cyprus, and this was as late as 1806. Such reflections in history remind us of the extreme discomfort endured by our ancestors and tilt the balance in disfavour of the "good old days".

Where the dark cluster of plantations of Phassouri thins out to make room for olive-groves, orchards and Limassol's famous vineyards, the castle of Kolossi rises in noble isolation.

It was already known in 1191 when Lionheart occupied the island, for it appears that Isaac Commenus, the Despot of Cyprus, maintained his camp on this spot. The present castle, recently restored to its original perfection, dates from the 15th century when the Grand Commander Louis de Magnac set his insignia on the castle's east wall: the royal quarters of Jerusalem, Lusignan, Armenia and Cyprus. Louis was succeeded in 1468 by an Englishman, John Langstrother, whose annual payment to the Treasury in Rhodes was fixed at four thousand ducats. Twenty years later, when Giorgio Cornaro prevailed upon his sister Queen Catherine to abdicate in favour of the Venetian Republic, he was rewarded by the grant of the fourteen villages which at the time composed the Commanderia and yielded a yearly income of eight thousand ducats. The Kolossi estates were confiscated on the Turkish conquest of the island in 1570, but the titular rank of Grand Commander of Cyprus remained in the Cornaro family till its extinction in 1799. By then the Kolossi sugar factory, which the Turks in turn exploited, had been put out of business by the rise of the West Indies sugar industry. Despite its Greek name, the castle of Kolossi is distinguished by architectural elegance and symmetry rather than size. Its function being military as much as domestic, the late Gothic keep, which is still reached by a drawbridge, constitutes the principal feature of the building. Some delightful details are to be seen inside, particularly the kitchen on the first floor and the fleur-de-lys carving of fireplaces in the two chambers of the uppermost storey, eloquent of kinship with masonry at Blois or Amboise in the château country of the Loire. The two upper floors are lit by fine round-arched windows while the crenellated terrace, which is open to the sky, has battlements and arrow-slits which Old Norse called *wind-eyes,* that expression from which we get our English "window". In the castle grounds stand two unusual structures, the old sugar factory which is now an open-ended shell, and a huge mediaeval waterworks. The latter consists of an aqueduct whose rushing stream still irrigates the lands of Kolossi and pours headlong from some magical reservoir in the hills.

Such water has enriched Limassol since the Middle Ages. Many a traveller has alluded to the mimosa, oleander, jasmin and pomegranates which grow half-wild in the southern valleys. During the 15th century local vines were so celebrated that the Portuguese chose them for the budding vineyards of Madeira. The soils of the two islands have given the descendants of the fructuous parent so contrasted a character that it would now be impossible to produce Madeira wine in Cyprus, and vice-versa. If the Lusignans and Venetians appreciated Cyprian wines, the Ottomans taxed it heavily to satisfy Muslim prejudice. The old rock-cut wine-presses became overgrown with scrub and, after many years of British indifference to viticulture, the Cyprus wine industry has recovered itself only in the last half-century. Even a casual visit to the wineries and distilleries of modern Limassol will indicate how seriously the gift of Dionysus is again regarded. And the same god confers his approval upon two annual occasions in Limassol, at Mardi Gras and the autumnal Wine Festival, when the libido is made respectably free.

Where under the sun do Biggin Hill and Middlesex Hill cultivate geraniums in winter and steak-and-kidney pudding in July? Where can a minister of the Church of Scotland play cricket on Sunday? The answer is at Episkopi, on the sinuous coast between Limassol and Paphos. Here an ancient village has lent its name to a Mediterranean overspill for the RAF – and stockbroker's daydream. Sociologists will be well occupied; escapists should drive past the regimented street openings and return to Cyprus in two miles, to the edge of the limpid sea at Curium.

Situated at Curium, which the Greeks call *Kourion* after the Kouris River, is one of the island's great classical sites. Herodotus claimed, on the strength of oral tradition, that Curium was founded by Argives. Certainly there were signs nearby of Achaean colonisation during the first wave of

Mycenaean expansion in the 14th century B.C. and of subsequent 12th century settlement after the onslaught of the
Dorians in Greece. Like Citium to the east, Curium's con-
nections in early history were with the Assyrian and Persian
Orient as often as with the Hellenes. The Levantine world
before Roman times was never so compartmented as school
atlases would suggest, and if King Stasanor of Curium de-
fected to Xerxes at the battle of Salamis in 498, his successor
Pasicrates aided Alexander the Great at the siege of Tyre.
In the 8th century B.C. the cult of Apollo was introduced to
Curium and this god pervades not only Curium but also the
Sanctuary of Apollo Hylates farther down the coast. Curium
itself takes the form of an acropolis overlooking the sweeping
shore. For archaeological purposes it was first explored by
di Cesnola in 1873; its outstanding buildings, however, the
Palace of Eustolios and the Theatre, were excavated only in
1933–48 and 1949–50, by the University of Pennsylvania.
The present theatre, restored in the 1960s, was a Roman
creation on an earlier Ptolemaic model. From its semi-circular
auditorium the Eumenides and the ghost of Banquo can be
heard to prosecute their vengeful courses. The palace, named
for one Eustolios, also originated in Roman days and its 5th
century mosaic floors and consummate bathing amenities
display a luxurious style of living.

Although Curium's acropolis commands the grander view,
the Sanctuary of Apollo Hylates is more evocative of the
divinity which sanctified the woodland place or *hyle*, of which
Apollo was traditional protector. Like the simple Shinto
shrines of Japan, the natural setting, in this case of pines and
cypresses, calls for meditation.

Over much of the Hellenic world, at Delos and Delphi in
Greece proper and at Didyma in Asia Minor, Apollo was
honoured with marmoreal splendour. The Cypriots on the
other hand showed small instinctive feeling for monumentality
and Apollo Hylates was, at Curium, worshipped as much in
the open air – in a forest which once abounded in deer – as

inside the small Temple of Apollo which, in its late first century Roman form, retires into the sacred groves. Such emphasis did not detract from the sanctity of the spot; Strabo records that he who dared lay an irreverent finger on the altar of Apollo was hurled from the chalky cliff at Curium into the jade waters. Everywhere formalised animism has that man's communion with nature, trees and plants have had an important part. The Celtic and Teutonic tribes attributed divinity to mistletoe, the Egyptians venerated the aloe, the heathen Greeks transferred their shamanistic allegiances to anthropomorphous deities but never outgrew, even in the Christian era, a certain attachment to trees. Nowadays in Cyprus the terebinth, a tree which bears turpentine, is at times seen decked with shreds of clothing. A person suffering from a chronic infirmity may make a pilgrimage to a tere-binth, there divesting himself of parts of his attire, praying all the while that he will likewise be stripped of his malady. The olive tree is yet revered in remoter places, for weary rustics will select its shade of a summer's afternoon because, they believe, evil genies are afraid to come near the whole-some, stalwart olive. The shade of the fig-tree is, on the contrary, conducive only to nightmares and for that reason no one will plant figs in his front-yard. Mere decades ago, olive twigs were burned in a pot which was then waved above the head of an approaching stranger, as a fumigation to ward off the evil eye. An interesting legend has to do with the tamarisk, a shrub which blooms very beautifully. It is said that when He was seized in the garden of Gethsemane Christ was tied to a tamarisk branch. He attempted to free Himself but the tamarisk proved unbreakable. Christ looking down upon it cursed it and condemned its blossom never to yield fruit. Some Cypriot peasants are therefore contemptuous of the shrub and refrain from using it as kindling wood. In certain villages the church may be laced in strands of thread designed to entangle malignant spirits, like hostile aeroplanes caught in barrage balloons.

East of Limassol the coastal plain broadens out towards Larnaca, and once one has passed through the rich suburbs there is little to commend to the visitor on the Nicosia highway before hitting Khirokitia. The road itself is often overburdened with fuming lorries carrying fodder, cement and lemonade bottles; its verge of stony beaches stands no comparison with the rest of the Cypriot coastline and one should either head for Larnaca and Nicosia or turn off to penetrate mountainous Pitsilia (Chapter 6) behind Limassol, which is not merely pastoral but a virtual novelty.

On the shore, or rather almost engulfed by the sea, the ruins of Amathus, whose pre-Christian chronology is unknown, are in the 20th century marked by no more than a tall bluff of masonry, a survivor of the harbour which once served a busy commerce. We know two things about Amathus. The first was the *Adonia*, or games held in commemoration of Adonis. Like the *Aphrodisia* at Paphos, these had for Cyprus the kind of meaning that the Olympic and Isthmian Games possessed for the people of Greece; they united all the people in feelings of a common identity and fate. On the first day of the *Adonia*, the women would celebrate Adonis' descent into Hades with wailing and weeping. On the second day, called Apparition Day, all the celebrants would break into dance and song in the conviction that the god was resurrected. The parallel with Christianity is obvious. Ritual worship included animal slaughter and, in remembrance of the boar by which Adonis perished, the pig was the usual victim. The second distinction of Amathus was to have given birth, in the 7th century A.D., to St John the Almoner, the first patron bishop of the Knights of St John and called Almoner by virtue of his public benefactions. His funeral at Amathus was attended by a miracle for, as his body was lowered into the episcopal tomb, the corpses of the two previous Bishops of Amathus who were interred there rolled aside to make way for the newcomer.

The colossal power-station of Moni, providing energy for

southern Cyprus, dominates the proximate shore. In two millenia from today will Moni appear in the guide-books as a monument of the Late Electric Age, traced by the thoughtful scholar to its historic antecedent, amber, which the Greeks called *elektron*?

CHAPTER NINE

Larnaca

*Khirokitia and neolithic Cyprus – Stravrovouni Monastery –
Lefkara – Dali and the death of Adonis – Ancient Citium –
Mediaeval and modern Larnaca – Cataclysmos – St Lazarus
Church – The Tekke of Hala Sultan – Salt Lake – Kiti
Church.*

Above electric pylons and the wondrous noise of internal
combustion, the excavation of neolithic Khirokitia on its
conical hill tells us about the oldest culture yet uncovered in
Cyprus, dating from about 5800 to 5250 B.C. Less ancient
than Jericho (which was a walled town as early as 8000 B.C.)
or the Anatolian settlement of Çatal Hüyük (6500 B.C.),
Khirokitia, which pre-dates neolithic southern Europe by eight
centuries, is evidence that the Stone Age Revolution, having
successfully substituted cultivation for hunting, and sedentary
pursuits for nomadism, had created a "primary village farmer"
economy and paved a direct way for the glories of the bronze
age. Like the early inhabitants of Asia Minor, the Eteo-
cypriots were brachycephalic, and the fact that they possesed
implements of obsidian, as well as flint, bone and andesite,
proves trading relations with the mainland, since obsidian
is absent from the geology of Cyprus. Some fifty dwellings
have been excavated; these, as is plain to see, consisted of a
circular room or *tholos,* built in beehive form of sun-baked
adobe and rubble. The *tholoi* housed both the quick and the

dead, for the latter were laid in simple pits dug in the floors. Here we receive a preview of the *tholos* tomb of Late Helladic times. At Mycenae, some four millenia away in the future, the famous beehive Tomb of Agamemnon entrenched in the Argive hillside and, indeed, the funerary customs at bronze age sites from Mesopotamia to Wessex, suggest a slow but supremely continuous evolution from those neolithic crossroads where man discovered his humanity.

At Khirokitia the dead were at best buried singly and in a contracted posture, often accompanied by gifts of tools, stone bowls and bead necklaces. Women were specially honoured in this way. In several *tholos* tombs a large quern was placed over the head or chest of the deceased, sure evidence that neolithic Cyprus feared the dead. Deer antlers and the bones of domestic animals found with human relics point to widespread animal sacrifice, and in one *tholos* there is a hint of child immolation—an eight-year-old lying face downwards with hands most probably tied behind his back. Infant mortality seems to have been general, for in one *tholos* alone twenty-five infants have been exhumed. The relics of other children and of young women trapped beneath monumental slabs indicate the kind of foundation rituals which are not extinct in the modern world. The Indian housebuilder of the Bolivian altiplano still imprisons a llama embryo in the base of his new dwelling and in many Muslim countries it is the custom to begin a great building project – such as the Aswan Dam – with an animal sacrifice. In the Late Stone Age bodies were interred outside the houses, one step towards the necropolis and the modern cemetery, but throughout the era the placing of heavy stones over the dead, and the persistence of gift-bestowal and sacrifice, signify simple belief in a life after death. At least four millenia before Jerusalem and Mecca became magnetic poles on the devotional compass, the curious positioning of the corpse, as at Khirokitia, in an easterly direction, is not easily explained. Were the dead expected to undertake a long journey towards the rising sun, origin of all life?

An outstanding example of Comnenian fresco art: the Pantocrator at Lagoudhera

The miniature
Church of St. James,
Trikomo

In the Karroo

The mysteries of birth and death have of course preoccupied every society and given rise to ceremonies no less elaborate today than in other epochs. The death of a Cypriot villager is a moment for communal grief and ritual, compounded of both Christian and pre-Christian elements. As soon as a man is deemed to be dying, he is removed from the bed-stead and laid upon a plain cloth on the floor. This is done so that he may die humble. After the body is taken away for burial, every water vessel of the house is emptied on the ground so that the soul of the deceased may be refreshed, an act reminiscent of classical libations. Orestes, for example, sprinkled water after the murder of Aegisthus. When a week has passed, a plate of *kollipha* (which, as we have seen, appears symbolically too on New Year's Day) and five loaves of bread are taken to the church where a memorial service for the deceased is performed. Afterwards the *kollipha* is shared by those present, who bless the departed soul, and the priest keeps the loaves as a reward for his intercessions. In the conservative household birth is also attended by ceremony. For instance, soon after delivery, the newborn child is covered with fine salt so that when it grows up it will be strong – hence the scornful adage, "You have not been well salted". On the occasion of the infant's first bath, seven almonds are dropped in the tub and then saved until baby acquires a decent set of molars.

From Khirokitia it is pleasant to follow the metalled road which forks left at Kophinou and to wind uphill through flaky chalk. From the eastern foothills of the Troodos the Capes of Kiti and Greco are seen protruding far out towards the hyacinth of sea and sky. Askew on its mountain pyramid, the Monastery of Stavrovouni commands the middle view, its eccentric position reminiscent of an ark left behind by the receding flood. Stavrovouni, or the "Mountain of the Cross" which lies just off the main thoroughfare from Limassol to Nicosia, takes its name from a fragment of the True Cross allegedly donated in the 4th century by the monastery's foundress, St Helena, whose philanthropy was proverbial.

Though Stavrovouni still maintains a small colony of monks, the *metochi* or dependencies of Ayia Varvara at the foot of the mountain accommodate larger numbers of brethren who expend daily energy on the cultivation of the terraces which gird the mountain. If the holy fragment has attracted generations of pilgrims to Stavrovouni, despite the hardships once involved in the ascent, the sacred relic was early incorporated in the chapel's own cross and we learn from one mediaeval visitor that this was "raised and suspended and nowhere attached". In Lusignan times, the monastery was inhabited by Latins as much as Greeks and it was not easy to distinguish between them. Felix Faber, a 15th century Dominican monk from Bavaria, was indignant to find a clerk at the monastery who knew no Latin and a monk at Ayia Varvara whom he would not have recognised from his dress, "for he wore a habit of camlet, and was curate of both the Greek and Latin churches, performing indifferently the office of either rite". Faber judged other aspects even less favourably. "Many Latin priests go over to the Greek rite and presume to take wives," he lamented, "but they wish at the same time to enjoy the privileges of Latin priests." "Small wonder," he continues, "that there is little religion in these remote places, which are never visited by the superiors of the order, where the monks are not corrected for their excesses and are even led astray by the iniquity of the Greeks." Such impressions, one hastens to add, are not made by today's tenants, for if the country priest is often the exemplary family man, celibacy is the rule in monastic life.

Proceeding north from Kophinou the hill villages of Lefkara suddenly loom deceptively close. From afar the higher village, Pano Lefkara, resembles a white and ice-blue fortress lit by a thousand windows and roofed in a flush of solferino – so tightly are its houses clustered around the campanile in the centre. Kato Lefkara below is a smaller version set at a less vertiginous angle. The Lefkaras are the historic hub of Cypriot lace-making, a fact which has visibly enriched them. It is

claimed that Leonardo da Vinci came here in 1481 to pur-
chase an altar-cloth for the Duomo of Milan. Certainly the
Venetians, who used Lefkara as a hill resort in summer, valued
the villagers' embroidery; Venetian tastes had an influence
on the design of the classic *lefkaritika* which is to this day
made by the women of Lefkara, who sit outdoors in sewing
circles, plying their needles in the ancestral fashion. There
is an equally long tradition of peddling the village's lace,
particularly in Aegean and Adriatic markets. Today the merchants of Lefkara deliver in bulk to city shops or else, like
spirited highwaymen, lurk in saloon cars on the outskirts of
the village to hail the foreign motorist as the latter suddenly
turns a bend.

In times past Lefkara was celebrated too as the source of
black medicinal gum called laudanum, collected from the
meadows and used as an antidote to plague. Produced by
dew falling on the leaves of a plant similar to sage, it was
gathered by a curious method. The peasants would drive their
goats to the pasture before sunrise so that they might browse
on the herb, for as laudanum is soft and sticky, it would
adhere to their beards, which were cut once a year and the
gum extracted by means of fire.

The shortest and slowest return to Nicosia is by a track
which no Lefkariot in his right mind would recommend. It
is a matter of crossing the final spur of the Troodos and
dropping down through Kornos to the main north-south axis.
It is also a matter of two hours' obstinate riding over exposed
rocks and twisting through some of the most savage, and
beautiful scenery in the island. A stream is crossed by a bridge
which commemorates the road's construction in 1923, by Sir
Malcolm Stevenson, the High Commissioner. In the twilight
the rubescent oozing earth, the jumble of boulders and carob-
trees, the giant fennels thrust like saffron umbrellas against
a tawny silhouette of monoliths, all proclaim the sustained
triumph of landscape. It is seldom that a goatherd, stray dog
or even a peevish magpie appear on this mineral-vegetable

stage. And on its far ridge, Lefkara recedes like a cloud vision of El Greco.

Beyond the ragged hamlet of Kornos the Mesaoria unfolds once more. The fertile plain is here interspersed with table-tops of sedimentary limestone, adding up to a kind of golf-course for the gods. Centuries of rain have eroded the lower layers of these mesas with the result that periodic upheavals of the uppermost strata have caused huge rocks to roll into the fairways. Geologists who explore among them may find fossilised shells, for the whole plain was once a sea-bed.

The soil of the Mesaoria has long been exceedingly fecund, for it was created by alluvia of chalk and gypsum washed down from the encircling bowl. Such deposits have supplied the main constituents for the growth of vines and cereals, and their beneficence is far from being exhausted.

In early summer the undulating fields are sheets of scarlet poppies, and these may have suggested to antiquity the blood of the dying Adonis. In any case the modern village of Dali, which luxuriates in the abundance of nature, is also the ancient Idalium where Apollo, Aphrodite and Athena were worshipped. Idalium never boasted a full-blown Greek temple but rather a *temenos* or open, rectangular sanctuary born of the Bronze Age and containing minor sacred buildings and several free-standing votive statues. One of the statues repre-sented Athena, who was also the Anaït of the Phoenicians. Her legend, like that of Adonis – and particularly his death – crossed the strait to enter Cypriot and Hellenic mythology. Let us look first at the archetypal Adonis of the Lebanon. To a point near Baalbek, where the River Nahr Ibrahim starts its short journey to the sea, the modern Lebanese, who are with the Maltese and Tunisians the most obvious heirs to Phoenicia, will direct the romantic traveller, for tradition has it that Adonis is wounded each spring in the same hills. Certainly when the river is at full flood, the waters run crimson. The death of the Cypriot Adonis may be less grandiose, but it is

still true that for many centuries Cypriot women came
annually to Idalium to mourn his fatal struggle with Hades
disguised as a boar. Where Hades' tears fell, anemones sprang
up, and these too are visible among the poppies.

In Byzantine days a great number of (mainly Roman)
fragments from the venerable city of Citium were assembled
to build a new town. Prominent among these was the *larnas*
or "cinerary urn", which gave the settlement the name of
Larnaca. Indeed half of early Larnaca rested upon the sarcophagi and urns of a Mycenaean and Phoenician past.
"Progress" at that time doubtless turned its back on historicism
and Citium was to lie submerged right up to the 1960s.
Founded by Achaeans from Argos and later occupied by
Phoenician colonists, Citium was famous in classical literature
as *Kition* and in the Hebrew scriptures as *Chittim*. At the
high noon of Hellenism, from the 6th century to the era of
Alexander the Great, Cyprus was a battleground between
Hellene and Semite – Salamis being the champion of Greek-
dom, while Citium and to a lesser degree Amathus usually
declared for the Phoenicians, Egyptians and Persians, whose
influence there was supreme. Archaeologists, under the eye of
Professor Karageorghis, have of late excavated certain zones
of Citium and most recently revealed a Phoenician temple of
the 9th century B.C. which, together with most of the city's
Phoenician monuments, was raised by the Ptolemies in the
late 4th century. A figurine of a seated goddess, probably
Astarte, many votive offerings and a treasure of Attic vessels
were unearthed in 1969 and this is merely a beginning. The
full story of Citium has thus yet to be recounted.

We know, however, that the names of two great men,
Cimon and Zeno the Stoic, were associated with Citium.
Memorials to both of them stand in the main square at
Larnaca. Cimon died offshore (449 B.C.) at the head of the
Athenian fleet, which consisted of two thousand triremes and
was designed to wrest the island from Achaemenid Persia. His
death was kept secret till victory had gone to the Athenians,

which gave rise to the saying : "Even dead he was victorious". According to Plutarch no man did more than Cimon to reduce the power of Persia.

Zeno, the founder of Stoicism (from *stoa*, "portico"), was born at Citium in 336 B.C. Having sustained, with characteristic forebearance, a shattering storm at sea, Zeno settled in Athens where he sowed his ideas on grammar, semantics, logic and ethics. In the latter domains his thought resembled that of Confucian and Taoist philosophy and anticipated Rousseau and Darwin, for his central principle was to live in accord with nature, within a universe ruled by *logos*. Since the *logos* in man originates from the universal *logos,* men are brothers by nature. Zeno died at 28. Objects from the golden days of Citium are exhibited in the new District Museum at Bamboula, a northern sector of Larnaca which is also the site of the old acropolis.

Mediaeval Larnaca had little conception of the city which lay beneath it; nor did it care much for the past. Its colonisation by western merchants in the Lusignan period made it susceptible to all manner of material favours once the Ottomans took power. The so-called Latins, a small but prosperous body of Catholics and Protestants who resided here and practically monopolised the island's foreign trade after the ruin of Venice, enjoyed both the privileges of the ancient régime and exemptions from the disabilities to which the Orthodox *rayahs* were liable. The Larnaca Latins, who were mostly descended from Frenchmen, Italians, Ionians, Syrians and Maltese, could in critical days depend upon the protection of Britain, France or some other power, and most of the European consuls in Ottoman Cyprus were chosen from among them. Their handsome houses have partially survived, and a surprising number of states, like the Scandinavian ones, still display their national seals above the door. But Larnaca, now the fourth town of Cyprus, is only a shadow of its former self. Ships are diverted to Famagusta or Limassol; tourism is undeveloped, and brave attempts by travel writers to liken the waterfront with its motley palms, telegraph wires and posters, to the resorts of the Riviera, are illusive. By way of a fetid nomansland, Athens Street extends into Ankara Street, to the Turkish quarter where the Ottoman citadel, built in 1625 on the Venetian model, is again "closed to visitors". (The Turks call the town *Tuzla*).

Still, Larnaca has the makings of a resort. Its prodigious history, its graceful architecture and seaside setting are simply in need of careful – and not too much – interpretation, editing and direction. Just once a year on Whit Sunday and Monday, the townspeople manifest a talent for showmanship. This is the seaside festival of *Cataclysmos,* which had its roots in the old Paphiot custom of celebrating Aphrodite's emergence from the spray, then later became linked in the popular mind with Noah's escape from the Flood and with the Feast of Pentecost. The feast of *Cataclysmos* starts with an ecclesiastic ceremony, the priest hurling a cross into the depths of the sea, whereupon the best swimmers of his congregation race one another to fetch it out. The winner is then blessed. Next there is a display of island commodities like Pitsilian nuts, oranges from Morphou and Lefka, Lefkara lace. Athletic contests are held and on Whit Monday music is made and various crafts stage their particular dances : the sickle dance, churn dance, butcher's dance and so forth.

Larnaca's most important monument is doubtless the Church of St Lazarus with its pale belfry and plainish walls. It is a large structure and historically prominent, for below the bema is an empty tomb once occupied, it is said, by Lazarus whom Christ had raised from the dead. Lazarus is believed by Cypriots to have spent the last thirty years of his second life at Larnaca, and to have been the first Bishop of Citium. His remains were transferred to Constantinople and later stolen and removed to Marseilles. Although his church was returned to Orthodox use after the Turkish conquest of Cyprus, the foreign community evidently retained such respect for it that its most striking features today are the memorials not only to Orthodox, but to Catholics and Protestants. In the porch there are 18th century funerary tablets in French, Italian and Greek; at the back a tidy Protestant graveyard contains the tombstones of English consuls and merchants who, says an early 19th century visitor, "had all died in the summer when the heat is excessive". Among them is the grave of the first American missionary to Cyprus, who died in 1839.

An excursion through the haphazard suburbs of Larnaca leads to two shrines which, in their own way, epitomise the religious spirit of the island's two main communities. Each embodies, respectively, Islam and Byzantine Christianity. The first beckons from its panache of palms on the Larnaca Salt Lake where the feathered tribe is again much in evidence. This is the Tekke of Hala Sultan, a temple with symbolic meaning for Sunni Muslims, one which pre-dates the Ottoman paramountcy by eight centuries, and a landmark on the south coast of Cyprus. The delicate etching of its minaret, its gentle cupola and fringe of ornamental flora far outshine the internal architecture, but the Tekke's sacred beginnings are themselves a special topic. Hala Sultan, from whom the Tekke receives its name, was foster-aunt of Mohamed. Though called at birth Rumeysa (Arabic for "bright-eyed lady") she was known to the prophet as Ummul Haram or, in Turkish, Hala Sultan, which means "respected mother". At a time when women, as nurses and concubines, joined their warrior menfolk in the forays of the great *jihad*, Hala Sultan took part in the first of twenty-four Arab invasions of Cyprus, in A.D. 647, until she tumbled from her mule, broke her neck and was given a martyr's burial at the place where now stands the shrine. Some say that her tomb was removed in 1760 by the Turkish custodian. At any rate the present Tekke was not erected till 1816, by Seyyit Mehmet Emin Effendi, who was Governor of Cyprus. Local claims that the Tekke is the third holiest place of Islam would be disputed by most Sunni as well as by most Shi'a Muslims, who are inclined to attribute such celebrity to Kerbela or Qum. It is so, nonetheless, that until Atatürk's Revolution the Tekke was saluted by all Turkish ships passing under the southern lee of the island and that till 1963 – when, ironically, the shrine was transferred to the custody of the (Greek) Cypriot Department of Antiquities – quite a traffic of pilgrims would be drawn hither during the feasts of Ramadan and Kurban Bairam. Today's Muslim peregrinations are made only by the Turks of Cyprus.

Swathed in perpetual twilight, the tomb itself is a trilithon which, in folklore, arrived from Mount Sinai borne on the wings of angels. With the Islamic clocks unwound and seldom an echo in its dank chambers, the Tekke has the air of an orphan compensated by a brilliant garden which, in this curious case, still belongs to the Turkish community. Here palms and lemon-trees crowd the saline lake-edge, watered from an independent source. By tradition the Salt Lake was the work of Lazarus, who, on his way to Larnaca, was consumed by thirst. Looking about him he saw a thriving vineyard on the spot of the present lake; then approaching a hut, he asked the owner of the vineyards, a selfish shrew of a woman, to give him a few grapes, but the woman, pretending that the vines had dried up that year, refused him refreshment. Lazarus indignantly cursed the hag and transformed the vineyard into a salt lake.

The visitor to Larnaca should on no account miss the Church of Panayia Angeloktistos at Kiti, some four miles west of the Tekke. If Kiti is called after Citium, whose refugees it may once have embraced, its renown stems from the Christian era, more precisely from that age immediately preceding the Arab invasions when Cypriot mosaic art was at its zenith. The church is entered by a narthex which once comprised a rib-vaulted Latin church, still well maintained. The naos, cruciform and domed, is of 11th century provenance. With its noble iconostasis, its handful of fine icons (notably that of the Archangel Michael) and a worthy fresco of St Bartholomew, Kiti church is good proof of the

Comnenian capacity for ecclesiastic art. But the 7th century mosaic composition in the conch of the apse is the highlight. Freer and more Hellenistic in feeling that the earlier mosaics at Kanakaria (Karpas), the Virgin, Child and Archangels here bear a lively relation to the 6th century mosaic portraits of Justinian and Theodora in the Church of St Vitale at Ravenna. However incomplete these restored masterpieces may be they are time and again invoked by Cypriot Greeks to bolster the historicity of Hellenic dominion of the island. Certainly when Kiti was built, the Cypriot Church was, next to the four original patriarchates of Constantinople, Alexandria, Antioch and Jerusalem, the senior of the autocephalous branches of Orthodoxy. The Emperor Zeno, after all, had bestowed on the island an Ethnarchy, or Archbishopric quite free of external authority, with prestige and privileges guarded to this day. When, for instance, Patriarch Benedict of Jerusalem visited President Makarios in 1969, he invested the Cypriot as "Grand Crusader of the Order of Orthodox Crusaders". The Archbishop in turn presented the Patriarch with a gold cross containing "a true piece from the Holy Cross". Thus while Greek Cypriots pay distant homage to their Homeric ancestors, a more truly filial devotion is accorded to Byzantium – which survives in so much more than the island's religion.

Before leaving the Larnaca district there is, on the Limassol road, another Ottoman monument of distinction, the Aqueduct of Bekir Pasha, built in 1745 during the Governorship of Ebubekir Pasha. Its flow, carried high on meandering masonry, used to supply the city of Larnaca in all but the severest drought. And at a short distance from its arches is a row of splendid century plants, descendants of that tree-like species, the *agave americana* which is native to Mexico. Sometimes attaining a height six times that of a man, the century plant lies low for some ten years and then one spring, for the first and last time, shoots forth yellow flowers resembling a candelabrum. The Turks are particularly fond of its decorative charms and have planted it in many a grave-yard.

To return to Nicosia there is an unencumbered route from Larnaca. Traversing first the familiar limestone tables of a freakish geology, it soon bounds across the wheat plain, passes beneath the vulgarian red roofs and neo-Byzantine churches of outer Nicosia and reaches Metaxas Square, exactly twenty-six miles from the Larnaca waterfront.

CHAPTER TEN

Famagusta and the Karpas Peninsula

The glories of mediaeval Famagusta – Churches, mosques and museums of the Walled City – Varosha and the Golden Sands – Birdcatchers of Paralimni – Ayia Napa and Cape Greco – Classical Salamis – Enkomi – Monastery of St Barnabas – The Karpas – Lefkoniko – Trikomo – Boghaz – Kantara Castle – Kanakaria Church – Ayios Philon – Untrodden sands – Apostolos Andreas Monastery and Cape Andreas

Few cities of mediaeval Christendom and none in the Near East save Constantinople enjoyed so illustrious a reputation as Famagusta. Out of the Crusader towns of Palestine, industrious fugitives from those Saracen victories which had culminated in the Fall of Acre poured into a sand-strewn Byzantine village across the strait and within two centuries established there a massive ring of fortifications, 365 churches and one of the greatest entrepôts for the oriental trade. Since Europe had yet to forge a sea route to India, Cyprus profited from many geostrategic and commercial advantages. To a Frankish, Genoese and Venetian overlordship, whose economic interests soon outweighed any religious ambition, Famagusta offered the most advanced facilities. Von Suchen, a German chronicler of the 14th century, observed one of the opulent Latins of this sea-port citadel who "betrothed his daughter, and the jewels of her head-dress were more precious than all the ornaments of the Queen of France", and went on to explain why this should be :

> Cyprus is the farthest of Christian lands, so that all ships and all wares, be they what they may and come they from what part of the sea they will, must needs come first to Famagusta, and in no wise can they pass it by; and pilgrims from every land journeying to countries over sea must touch at Cyprus. And daily from the rising of the sun to its setting are heard rumours and news; and the tongues of every nation are heard and read and talked.

The consuls of Genoa (from 1372 till 1464) and of Venice (till the Ottoman conquest) were the real magnates of Famagusta and upon their acumen depended the political fortunes of western rule in Cyprus. Shakespeare located his *Othello* in "Venice and a Cypriot sea-port", with his main protagonist surrounded by Gentlemen of Cyprus and with the luckless Desdemona slain in a tower which, naturally enough, has its enduring counterpart in the city of our day, namely the Citadel.

The wall of Famagusta is almost intact and one can walk around it. The Venetian bastions which bear Italian names are also belvederes giving on one side to the harbour, the earthworks and the new town, and on the other to the shadow of a Latin glory. The Citadel, commonly called Othello's Tower, is akin to 14th century castles stretching from the Celtic marches of Britain to the Hanseatic ports of the Baltic, for it follows a classic pattern of square keep and circular towers placed at the four corners.

From 1570 to 1571 Famagusta was besieged by the Turks, and its loss to them is one of the most vivid passages in mediaeval chronology. Defended by a mere seven thousand Venetian troops under their General, Mark Anthony Bragadino, this, the most redoubtable of Cypriot forts, sustained ten months of siege until its garrison fell prey to sickness and starvation. On the 5th August 1571, in the very year when

Don John of Austria repelled the Turkish navy from more westerly waters, General Bragadino, accompanied by his lieutenants Baglioni, Martinengo and Quirini, went to the Ottoman camp and was politely received by Lala Mustafa Pasha. After the delivery of keys and when Bragadino had risen to take his leave, Lala Mustafa demanded special hostages for the safe return from Crete of the Turkish vessels which were to convey him and his men to the forthcoming campaign in that island. Bragadino refused this on the ground that the terms of his surrender had not alluded to such an item. Mustafa now accused the Venetian of bad faith, and of having put to death fifty Turkish pilgrims after he had surrendered, a charge which was vigorously denied by Braga-dino. In a rage the Pasha handed the four Venetians over to executioners, and in a few minutes, Baglioni, Martinengo and Quirini were dismembered under the eye of their commander-in-chief, for whom a more horrible death was reserved. Lala Mustafa ordered the Jewish executioner to sever the General's nose and ears. Three times Bragadino was made to lay his head upon the block as if to be executed, then, heavily chained, was thrown into a shadowy dungeon and left for nine days in that condition. On the tenth, by order of Mustafa, whose calculated violence bordered on psychosis and earned him the disrespect even of his own people, Bragadino was brought from prison and forced to carry earth for the repair of the fortifications after which, more dead than alive, the courageous soldier was tied to a stake and, in Mustafa's gloating presence, was flayed. His skin was stuffed with straw and set on a cow. In bitter mockery the red umbrella under which the living Bragadino had ridden to camp was held over it while the stuffed body was paraded through the streets. The skin was then despatched with the heads of the other three Venetians as gifts to the Sultan. Many years afterwards Bragadino's brother and sons purchased it at high cost and laid it to rest at Venice, in the Church of SS. Giovanni e Paolo.

Death and desecration accompanied Mustafa's triumph. The graves and icons of the Cathedral of St Nicholas, the city's prime symbol of Latinism, were scientifically ravaged, its frescoes whitened, its ogival glass windows converted to fretted arabesques, all in the name of the Prophet.

Modelled on Rheims by craftsmen brought from Champagne, this 14th century masterpiece soon grew a minaret, iwans and mihrabs and became known as Lala Mustafa Mosque, a name it preserves to our day. Before we return too harsh a judgment on the Turks, it is worth recalling that the Latins were capable of equal intolerance and callous despoliation. In 1204, to take but one example, the western Crusaders outdid the Visigoths and Vandals in the treasure-chest of a Constantinople won from the Greeks. Venting their hatred of Orthodoxy, the self-appointed guardians of western civilisation (notably the Franks) entered the greatest church of eastern Christendom, smashed its silver iconostasis, burned the holy books and seated upon its patriarchal throne a besotted harlot who sang lewd verses as they drank from the lustrous chalices. Not to mention the murder of clerics, violation of nuns and indiscriminate plunder.

From the exterior, at least, the Mosque's original function is abundantly clear, and for all the incongruity of the Muslim superimpositions there is, in the natural effulgence of Cyprus, something to be said for them. The clerestory, rib-vaults, buttresses and rose-windows are the work of a purely northern genius, designed for temperate contexts, and while the Gothic style suits the Abbey at Bellapais to perfection, maybe by virtue of the lush and strongly vertical vegetation which enfolds it, at Famagusta the Cathedral of St Nicholas must have appeared more fitting when all about it were other buildings in the western spirit.

A walk to the remaining churches, mostly reduced over four centuries, will nourish the imagination. Close to the Citadel the ruins of St George of the Latins' Church (late 13th century) recalls St Denis and the early flowers of Gothic in France. The remains of a 13th century Franciscan church and the façade of the Venetian Palazzo del Proveditore (with its arcade compiled of columns brought from Salamis) stand in the centre of the walled town. To the Palazzo the 19th century liberal playwright and poet Namik Kemal was exiled by a Sultan who feared the revolutionary implications of a play, *Vatan yahut Silistre* ("Silistria the other Fatherland"), which he had staged in Istanbul. Namik Kemal is a national dramaturge of the Turks, and his bust stands outside.

In better shape is the 14th century Church of St Peter and St Paul, used for centuries as a mosque and now as a warehouse. In the north-eastern quarter are the husks of the Armenian and Nestorian churches, the latter serving as the Greeks' own church (Ayios Yeoryios Xorinos or St George the Exiler) till in 1964 the entire Greek community abandoned the old city to the Turks, who now call it their own. So total is their occupancy that the colour blue seems to be reserved for the sky. One is reminded of Kitchener's observation about the Turks a century ago. "They prefer," he said, "white-and-red striped Manchester stuffs for their clothes, whereas the Greeks are almost always dressed in blue indigo-dyed stuffs of home manufacture".

Famagusta-within-the-Walls is doubtless a livelier place than it was two centuries ago when the population had dwindled to three hundred. In those days the occasional Christian visitor was forbidden to enter it on horseback or to cross the threshold of Lala Mustafa Mosque. Fearing forcible conversion to Islam, simpler Greeks stayed away. The old town had been left in ruins and ceased to be militarily effective. Hasselqvist the roving Swede noted two hundred cannon, not one of which was serviceable. The Turkish garrison, called *Levanti*, constituted the "worst troops that the Grand Signor has in his pay". For years Famagusta was an ideal repository for the Sultan's undesirables, Namik Kemal among them. It was considered ultra-provincial by the standards of Istanbul. A result of physical isolation from

Anatolia is that Turkish Cypriots still speak a purer Turkish, freer from Arabic and Persian borrowings, than the metropolitan Turk of the mainland. Mediaeval Famagusta also provided a ready quarry of stones, as the engineers of the Suez Canal were to discover. Considering these trials, the old city retains a surprising veneer of nobility. Look at the sturdy Land Gate rearing from its moat and you confront one of man's more indestructible works.

The Greeks' name for Famagusta is *Ammochostos,* "buried in the sand," a decreasingly apt description of the city, even of the modern town of Varosha which has transformed what maps once designated as "plantations of madder" into a major resort of the Mediterranean, and certainly the most swinging in Cyprus. Indeed Famagusta now benefits from the islands' most popular beach, the best harbour and the fastest road to Nicosia. Its Golden Sands are enlivened all year by the attributes of modish bathing resorts, which means parasols and the sun cult, skin-diving and water-skiing in translucent water. Speed-boat races mark the summer season; sailing regattas are the rule on winter Sundays. Swimming is safe – except on those rare stormy occasions when it is better to settle under a eucalyptus with a bottle of ouzo. Neither jelly-fish nor sharks – those scourges of the north and south – trouble the Cypriot coast, and humankind has still to invade the Golden Sands in a horde. The sea-front is in the course of change. Haphazard speculation in the early 1960s has ceded to a cosmopolitan order of glass and fibres. Sports cars and clubs put an accent on youth. Varosha is already a residential town in its own right, and rather selective in its preferences.

Greek-speaking "society", which has settled in Varosha, keeps up the Lusignan habit of the King and his barons. Unlike Nicosia or Limassol, where entertaining is more democratic, Famagusta's social roll contains little more than three hundred privileged. Half of these may be invited to a party one evening; the rest will follow next week. Creative culture is amazingly vital for so small a city. Painters and musicians have assembled, since the First Pancyprian Exhibition of Arts and Crafts in Coronation Year (1953), on various occasions. The Famagusta District Museum in Varosha, where Salamis and Enkomi and Byzantine church art from the Karpas are well represented, is a workshop for modern primitives. But the archaeological marvels of the district are but a few miles away and can be experienced directly.

Before turning north to explore them one should excurse south to Cape Greco, into a treeless and sunfilled country where the windmills and sunflowers and perpetual seascape bring to mind the Aegean isles. From time unrecorded the peninsula has furnished a landing stage for birds of passage. And since the Venetians acquired a taste for pickled warblers, the village of Paralimni has never been out of business. The Latins named the hapless species *beccafico* and *becquefigue*. The Greeks call it *ambelopoulia* or "birds of the vineyard". At Paralimni there are still Papagenos who lime their trees in preparation for the catch. In September and October some five thousand fat and heavy migrants passing south through the island end up in vinegar. During spring the catch drops sharply because the birds are lighter, and thus more agile. The pages of *The Times* have lately registered Anglo-Saxon indignation at the restoration of this practice in Italy. It is argued that the balances of nature demand the conservation of little birds in life rather than pickle; in the case of Paralimni the rate of casualties is probably too low to disturb the natural laws of survival. But unless one nurtures a passion for their flesh (and bones), humanitarianism appeals to all *beccaficos* to change their passage – or else Paralimniots to concentrate on sunflowers.

As one rides across the ozonic slopes of the cape beyond Paralimni, the terrain resembles more and more those windy parts of Crete. Dozens of windmills, driven by the *livas,* draw water for the vineyards and wheatfields which cleave to the shore. Farther on a limestone outcrop signals Cape Greco, round which green waters run. Near the sea crouch the unusual Church of Ayia Napa and its monastery, now un-inhabited but still intact. Done in pinkish stone, Ayia Napa exemplifies Venetian influence at its provincial best. A slim campanile, whose bell-rope rests on the rock from which some of the church is carved, offsets the squareness of the outlying buildings. Roofed with two barrel vaults to which one can climb from the outside, the church is graced with ogees and candelabra. Guarded by a solid gatehouse, the courtyard outside contains a beautiful fountain, whose water spouts from the four volutes of an Ionic column. This faint reflection of glittering Venice was one of the republic's last gifts to the Levant, as year by year the Ottoman tide swept Venetian ships to safer seas.

Midway up the Bay of Famagusta, where the sands curve to the hazy blue backbone of the Karpas, the most imposing city of classical Cyprus has its foothold. Until the 1950s, most of Salamis was embedded in a thicket, although its remains had been rediscovered in 1882. Now, thanks to the endeavours of Professor Karageorghis and others, the grandeur of Salamis lives again in its setting of eucalyptus, pines and marigolds. It was founded, it is said, by Teucer, the brother of Ajax, and named by him after the island of the Saronic Gulf off which the Athenians were destined to rout Xerxes.

Salamis was colonised both from Anatolia and the Pelop-ponese. After centuries of Assyrian, Persian and Phoenician rule, the Achaean tradition asserted itself in the person of Evagoras who, claiming descent from Teucer, inaugurated a half-century of enlightened despotism of a kind which is often invoked by Cypriot Hellenes as a golden age. Certainly there were intimate ties with Greece, and Cyprian Salamis was known to Athens. In Euripides' play *Helen* (412 B.C.), Teucer tells Helen that he will to "Cyprus isle, where Phoebus hath foretold that I shall dwell, and on the walls I raise I shall bestow the name of Salamis in memory of that dear country that I have left behind". Indeed its repute was greater then than today. Quite a few tourists pronounce "Salamis" as if it were an Italian sausage.

After the death of Alexander the Great, who had wrested the island from the Persians, Ptolemy's ally Nicocreon ruled the whole of Cyprus from Salamis until, accused of dealing with Ptolemy's enemies, he burnt himself to death. In 1966 Karageorghis discovered what may have been the King's pyre. Under Roman aegis, a cosmopolitan community established itself. From among its Hebrew denizens Barnabas was born, and it was to his former co-religionaries that St Paul preached in the year 45. The Jews of Salamis actually rose up against the appointees of Trajan, in A.D. 116, and decimated the Graeco-Roman population. And it is interesting to note that at the outset of our century Theodor Herzl for a time contemplated setting up the Jewish State not in Palestine but in Cyprus.

Salamis was struck by earthquake in the year 76 and again in 332 and 342, on which latter date a tidal wave devastated the port. The Emperor Constantius II, who esteemed the Salamine Church, relieved the survivors of taxation, rebuilt the town and called it Constantia. So strengthened, it fast superseded Paphos as the Cyprian capital and flourished thus till, in 647, the Emir of Muslim Syria at the head of an Arab flotilla besieged and captured it, and slaughtered most of the Salamines. The same story was re-enacted six years later, and the ruins of Constantia sank beneath mountains of sand.

Roman, and to a lesser degree Hellenistic and Byzantine, relics dominate Salamis in its substantial restoration. The magnificence of the original Gymnasium, ranged around its Roman palaestra, is envisaged from the walls and Corinthian columns which again encompass it. In its northern annex, which once included a swimming pool, antiquarians have set nine out of the fifty-odd statues which have come to light. That these nine, which date from the 2nd century, should be headless is the mark of early Christian intolerance. Rome's vast obsession with bathing is obvious from the sluices, runnels and basins which line the adjoining block. An aqueduct brought water from the spring at Kythrea. One wonders if the Salamines (or indeed the people of Leptis or Pompeii) ever took advantage of the seductive sea lapping at their doors. The Theatre has been rebuilt since its discovery in 1959. This building, a model of the Augustan epoch, naturally follows the pattern of the Greek hemicycle. In its orchestra, for instance, the priest would sacrifice to Dionysus before a performance. From its decayed proscenium, sculptures of Apollo and the Muses have been recovered, together with a tablet honouring the good works of Hadrian. If the mood of Salamis is imperial, the location is sylvan. Pillars and broken pedestals are laced with the greenery of the giant fennel, whose spring flowering brings forth a cascade of yellow. In autumn its stalks are used by Famagusta fishermen as lamp-stands for night fishing, and according to myth Prometheus bore the fire stolen from heaven inside its resilient stem.

Stasinos the poet, Evagoras the warrior king and Barnabas the saint were natives of Salamis. Living there in the 8th century B.C. Stasinos based his epic *Cypria* on the Greek world as it was before the Trojan War. His Cyprus lay in the dim but recognisable shadow of Mycenae. Sparse and monumental like the palace of Tiryns, his language is the Homeric of Argos. The everyday Greek tongue of modern Cyprus is the demotic of the mainland – the official language the purist (*katharevousa*) form of Greek, but the Cypriot dialect, which is barely intelligible to an Athenian, is akin to the ancient Homeric idiom of Arcadia – whence the first Hellenes reached the island. If sprinkled with western and Turkish expressions, its shape and spirit are authentic. So too the rustic plough (where it has not ceded to the 20th century), which is the plough mentioned by Hesiod. So too the art of carving motifs on gourds, so beloved of the tourist, which Early Bronze Age potters transferred to their water-jars. Likewise rural methods of baking bricks, of dancing and singing. To this ancestral habit add the force of Greek education and you will understand why Cypriot Greeks count themselves as descendants, not only of Stasinos, but of Homer. And you will then sense that Cypriot writing is but a part of Greek writing, individualistic notwithstanding. The 15th century chronicles of Leontios Makheras, for example, are composed in a popular style corresponding to the spoken language of the Frankish period. But Makheras is a writer for all Greeks. Evagoras, the second notable Salamine, lives in the Cypriot memory as the incarnation of Greek resistance and precursor of Dighenis. As for "Joses, who by the apostles was surnamed Barnabas, a Levite, and of the country of Cyprus" (*Acts IV*) he was interred near the Royal Necropolis of Salamis (where in the 8th century B.C. human and horse sacrifices were still in evidence). Without the discovery of his relics, the Cypriot Church would be poorer in privilege. The short biblical passages relating the saint's journey with Paul are amplified by Cypriot folklore, ever imaginative. Barnabas, it happens, was a puritan. At Curium he objected so strongly to the nudity of the city's athletes that a mountain tumbled down and killed all the pagans. Rising over the saint's supposed grave, the Monastery of St Barnabas is served by a two-domed church where three aged monks, blood brothers, turn out icons at a professional pace. In their blue cassocks and with white hair neatly knotted at the nape they are a magnificent species. From the monastery walls the faces of King Paul, Queen Frederika and *Strategos* Grivas peer out as if nothing had happened.

More than any revelation in the island, the discovery of a complete late bronze age city, at Enkomi (near Salamis), affirms the Mycenaean impact on Cyprus in Helladic times. The first investigations here were made by British Museum expeditions at the end of the 19th century. In 1896 a number of tombs yielded excellent Mycenaean pottery and wrought metals. These are now installed in Bloomsbury where, on a rainy afternoon, the Londoner can glimpse something of that resplendent age (1600–1000 B.C.) which is recaptured in the *Iliad*.

It was the turn of the Swedes under Gjerstad in 1930 to start systematic digging in the grassy plain where Enkomi lies. A hoard of Mycenaean riches, in particular ceramics, pointed to Argive trade. The question of whether the Cypriots imported Mycenaean ware or made it for themselves after the fashion of the mainland, is a subject of debate no less spirited than that which rages over the original name of Enkomi. In 1934 the French archaeologist Claude Schaeffer came to Enkomi to test his theory that the Canaanite city of Ugarit (modern Ras-Shamra), which he had just excavated, was intimately tied to Mycenae. His work at Enkomi, supplemented by that of Porfiriof Dikaios, has continued at intervals ever since and vividly confirms the link not only with the Greek cities of the Achaeans but with Ugarit, which was settled by Argives.

It is scarcely surprising that Mycenae's commerce with far-flung points like Ugarit and the Hittite capital of Bogazköy should have touched Cyprus. And it should not astound us if Enkomi were identified with the Alasia of Hittite and Egyptian texts. We know from the latter that the kings of ancient Alasia – which certainly betokened a Cyprian city or even the island itself – shipped copper to the Pharaohs. Schaeffer's mind is made up, and he insistently refers to "Enkomi-Alasia". Other scholars, like Karageorghis, equate Alasia with Citium, which lay closer to the copper mines. In any case this is food for the adventurous school of "diffusionists" who are happiest when Ming ceramics are exhumed in East Africa, when Peru and Polynesia are separated by no more than a balsa-raft sea voyage.

Professor Schaeffer and his team tend to labour in the cool season, but there are scarved women who continue all the year, cutting away at the bright and rampant flora. A wooden caravan follows them about and is so far the only salient on the landscape, since the city is still being unwrapped from its padding of earth. The result is already handsome.

After its robust beginnings in the third millenium, when it

traded with Syrians and Egyptians in metals, Enkomi was transfigured by Mycenaean merchants and colonists who, in the 16th and 13th centuries B.C. made it an intermediary between the Aegean and their Syrian emporia. Though it is laid out in a regular grid that would gladden a Texan town-planner, the architecture of Enkomi never attempted the grandeur of Mycenae itself but specialised in skilful execution and refinement of detail. Its treasures of bronze and pottery, gold and silverplate, now piling up in the vaults of the Cyprus Museum, are proof of an energetic Mycenaean culture in which native and Achaean elements are sometimes fused and sometimes coexistent. The elegant 12th century bronze statue of the Horned God (Apollo?) unearthed by Dikaios, exemplifies fusion. But some 13th century pottery is purely Mycennaean.

There is something else. Two tablets bearing Cypro-Minoan characters are suddenly the object of speculation. Their decipherment could throw light on Enkomi and Alasia, and even more. A lady from Dublin declares she has decoded one of them, and is convinced that it recounts how Ajax and his brother Teucer (the founder of Cyprian Salamis) helped themselves to spoils in an episode of the Trojan War. Applying shorthand techniques and wartime experience of ciphers, Beatrice Gwynn is eager to see the other tablet, which is under study by the French and is as closely guarded as moonstones. If she is right, her text may not only be a flash on the unlit road from Middle Minoan hierglyphics to the earliest Greek alphabet, but also vindicate those who hold that Homer used newsworthy inscriptions like these as archives for the *Iliad* and *Odyssey*. Miss Gwynn, what next?

The excitement of current excavation is real enough. One forgives di Cesnola. When a tomb is opened, the stench of air-tight relics is sensed by the nose as distant stars are perceived with the eye across millenia. Ceramic objects are removed at once, but the skeletons are left. Perhaps to scare tourists.

From a point near Antiphonitis a full sixty miles of bony highland prolongs the northern spine of Cyprus by means of a tail, the Karpas. This is followed by a highway and whether one starts at Famagusta or sets out across the Mesaoria through the immaculate lace-making village of Lefkoniko, the journey brings mile after mile of visual rewards. If one approaches from Kyrenia there is too the eastern stretch of the Forest Road winding around the Mount Olympus of Durrell's "Gothic Range" and reaching at last Kantara Castle, which, as its Arabic name suggests, crowns a sharp escarpment above the sea. Kantara in history is almost a carbon copy of Buffavento, except that today it enjoys a better condition and commands a double view of the Mediterranean. Not only the Taurus but sometimes the Lebanon Mountains smudge the violet horizon.

WELCOME TO GRIVAS DIGHENIS' BIRTHPLACE proclaims the sign in divers tongues (including Russian) at the entrance to Trikomo. The hero of the EOKA campaign was indeed born here, in 1898, and is now retired in Athens. Those who see him only in the guise of a guerrilla chieftain should sample the Grivas memoirs – and photographs of Grivas the courtly civilian. At Trikomo there is a tiny chapel, named Ayios Yakovos for St James, sitting in the main square. In the configuration of a 15th century Greek cross it unfailingly charms its visitors. The late Queen Marie of Romania, for instance, ordered a replica of it to be built on the coast of the Dobrogea.

Spring garnishes the meadows, the olive trunks and plots of maize with a milliard wild flowers, and the flaming earth is responsive to man. At the alfresco resort of Boghaz snails are abundant enough to feed the island's gastronomes. At Koma tou Yialou painted caïques gleam on the midday sand while their owners cool off with beer at the new taverna. New nets, new harbour, new road; the Karpas is not the forgotten appendix it might appear on the map.

Lythrangomi deserves its pilgrims. In the conch of its central apse, the Church of Panayia Kanakaria has a 5th or

6th century mosaic picture of the Virgin and Child, attended by Archangels. As the oldest mosaic in the island it is fragmentary, having suffered from Saracen pillage. In the south porch an icon of the Virgin of Kanakaria (15th century) inherits from an earlier composition the legend that a Saracen, on shooting an arrow at the picture, drew blood. After the Ottoman conquest a Turk replaced the Arab. . . . A few decades ago another icon in this church was credited with rain-compelling power. If there had been a drought the villagers assembled at sunset and the priest would take the icon from the iconostasis. Once the whole congregation had walked to a chapel on the shore and prayed there for divine intercession, the icon would be dipped thrice into the waves, and by the time it had regained its usual place, rain clouds should have filled the sky. Did they abandon this ceremony because the clouds forsook them, or did Lythrangomi update its water system?

After Yialousa, a big warm village spread over a hill, the surface of the Karpas – well-tilled, fertile and inhabited – is engraved on the eye. The rural inhabitants themselves are often invisible, but we are reassured by their bleached cottages, the dovecotes, the gardens of cactus and geraniums, the island dog (of an aristocratic breed not unlike a mottled Dalmatian) and the outdoor brick-stoves where young goats like to perch. The bucolic joy denied to industrial societies, such as lunching under a tree while your mule is tethered aside and your wife draws water, is granted everyone in this peninsula.

We are in Rizokarpaso, a town of material affluence – which means modern banks and a sugary neo-Venetian church. To the north, where palms reach down to a rock-strewn cove, the derelict Church of Ayios Philon stands as memorial to the Byzantine city of Carpasia, burnt by the Arabs in 802. Its fine mosaic pavement justifies a détour and no doubt too the *kafeneion* which adjoins the church.

Both coasts of the Karpas consist by turn of dunes, rock-shelves and cliffs. Sometimes a carpet of dwarf pines unrolls to the shore : firs, fennel and aromatic bushes embellish the interior. Beaches are so unfrequented that they remain without names and the most spectacular of them, which lies beyond the rounded gypsum hills called the Khelones, has been popularly named "Pachyammos" – like a dozen others. Here the dunes form a sloping tongue of sand between the scrub and iridescent bay. This is bathing as if bathing had just been invented.

Where the cartographers draw an acute angle in the sea, thus marking the eastern extremity of Cyprus, a belfry and caravanserai denote the Monastery of Apostolos Andreas, so lonely a shrine that pilgrims must be accommodated for days at a stretch. They arrive in buses, taxis and venerable Austins and follow the clockwork movements of the priest and archi-mandrites as the latter revolve about the big church during *esperinos*. Visibly afflicted with paralysis, a wizened old woman kisses each icon with an adhesive strength and abases herself on all fours. Though moderns frown on the practice, wax effigies of the suffering are carried to church as a tangible prayer for health. Resembling so many caramels in an expensive confectionery, the effigies may be as large as life. A wax figure with walking stick indicates a lame supplicate. Bulging stomachs suggest something more commonplace. Parents of children who are late in learning to talk hang a wax model of the infant tongue before the icon of St John the Evangelist, who is Cypriot patron of the spoken word. A musty chapel on the cliff covers the churning wells which, they say, refreshed Andrew the Apostle on a voyage. Never distant from the islander's mind or eye and constantly forging his history, the sea forces a passage around Cape Andrew and is liberated. In the phrase of Euripides :

> Where is the home for me?
> O Cyprus, ensconced in the sea.

CHAPTER ELEVEN

Useful Information

This chapter is divided into four sections: Travel to Cyprus, Travelling in Cyprus, Accommodation and General Information. It is intended only to be a brief guide, and fuller information on any point can be obtained from one of the tourist offices listed below.

UK	Cyprus Trade and Tourist Centre 211–213 Regent Street London W1
USA	Embassy of Cyprus 2211 R. Street, Northwest Washington 11, DC
France	Ambassade de Chypre 23 Rue de Galilée Paris 16°
Germany	Tourist Office Zypern Bethmannstrasse No 50–54 Frankfurt-am-Main 1
Greece	Embassy of Cyprus 4 Zalokosta Street Athens
Egypt	Embassy of Cyprus 3 Sharia Badrawi Ashur Dokki Cairo

* * *

TRAVEL TO CYPRUS

Air: Fifteen airlines call regularly at Nicosia, including Cyprus Airways, BEA, BOAC and Olympic Airways. Direct flights from London Heathrow are frequent, and, once there, connecting flights to other Mediterranean and Near Eastern countries are excellent. Any travel agent will supply exact times and fares.

Sea: There are no scheduled passenger sailings from the United Kingdom but regular sailings go

154

from Marseilles (Zim Navigation Co), Venice (Epirotiki and Typaldos lines), Trieste (Adriatica line), Brindisi and Piraeus (Kavounides) and many ports in the Near East. In addition a number of cruises call at Cypriot ports and travel agents and steamship companies will supply details.

Passports and Visas: Valid passports are necessary of course, but UK citizens and citizens of the following countries do not need visas: Belgium, British Commonwealth, Denmark, Finland, France, Federal Republic of Germany, Greece, Iceland, Ireland, Italy, Liechtenstein, Luxembourg, Netherlands, Norway, San Marino, Spain, Sweden, Switzerland, USA and Yugoslavia. Those wishing to stay in Cyprus for more than three months should apply to the Immigration Officer, Nicosia, for a permit.

Health: Although the island is healthy and no special vaccinations are needed it is as well to take out medical insurance before going, as the social insurance scheme does not extend to foreigners.

TRAVELLING IN CYPRUS

Buses and Taxi Services: Most towns and villages are connected by bus and taxi services. The intertown buses run until the evening but the country buses fit their schedules to a peasant way of life taking villagers to market in the morning and returning at midday. Cheap taxi services also run regularly between the main towns and to the hill resorts. Seats are booked in advance and the cost is approximately 200 mils for 25 miles (4s). Information on these services may be obtained from the Tourist Information Bureaux, the

addresses of which are given in the final section of this chapter.

Taxis: In the towns there is a flat rate of 200 mils (4s) for 2 miles. For longer distances payment is by time and is approximately 700 mils an hour. If a taxi is being taken for a whole day then a special arrangement should be made. The cost should be about £3 10s 0d to £4 10s 0d. As there are no taxi ranks one must walk to the nearest taxi office or telephone. Your hotel will advise on this.

Car Hire: Numerous firms specialise in self-drive car hire. Prices range from 2,000 mils (40s) for a small car up to 3,000 (60s) for a large one. These rates apply for unlimited mileage for one day: reduced rates are applied for longer periods. Good road maps are available from most bookshops. International licences are accepted but a temporary Cyprus driving licence can be obtained for 500 mils without difficulty on the strength of a valid national driving licence. Petrol costs between 4s 2d and 4s 6d per gallon, depending on the grade.

ACCOMMODATION

Hotels: A new list of hotels is published annually in a brochure available free from Tourist Offices and travel agents: full details of class and price are given. Prices are very reasonable: Full board for one person in a double room would cost a little over £5 in a luxury hotel, about 65s in a 1st class hotel and 45s in a 2nd class hotel.

Villas and flats: These may be hired for periods of over a month at rents varying between £20 and £60 per month. Most rented accommodation is to be found in or around Nicosia, Famagusta and Limassol but villas can also be found in the mountains and near Kyrenia. The Tourist Information Bureaux issue lists of agents dealing in villas and flats.

Camping: Camping is allowed anywhere in Cyprus provided that permission is obtained from the District Officer. There are no proper camp sites except for one on Mount Troodos in a pine forest 5,700 feet above sea level.

Youth Hostels: There are four youth hostels: at Nicosia, Paphos, Limassol and Troodos. For further information apply to The Cyprus Youth Hostels Association, P.O. Box 1328, Nicosia, Cyprus.

GENERAL INFORMATION

Ancient Monuments and Museums: The Department of Antiquities administers most ancient monuments and museums and is based on the Cyprus Museum in Museum Street, Nicosia. Entrance fees are usually between 50 and 100 mils and leaflets on the sites may be purchased from the custodian for 50 mils. Full sets may be purchased at the entrance to the Cyprus Museum. Students and architects may obtain free passes to all sites and museums by applying at the Department. It is worth remembering that all are shut on public holidays. For monuments and sites under Turkish Cypriot control the Cyprus Turkish Tourism Department, 29 Selim II St., Nicosia, is the best source of information.

Cigarettes: Local cigarettes are 2s for 14; foreign cigarettes can be obtained at rather higher prices.

Climate: Summer is long, dry and very hot but the heat is mitigated somewhat by the dry air and, on the coast, the sea breezes. Temperatures on the plains in August often go up to 100°F. The winter is mild, the daily mean temperature being 50°F inland in January. The sea is always warm: 61.4°F in January, 79.4°F in July. What little rain there is comes in winter. The Troodos mountains, due to their height, have a much cooler climate, with higher rainfall, again, mainly in winter. In the summer temperatures will be some 20°F lower than in Nicosia and in January and February there is enough snow to support a thriving winter sports industry. Spring and autumn are the best times to visit Cyprus, especially if a certain amount of sightseeing is envisaged: the sun and the sea are then quite hot enough for the average Anglo-Saxon!

Clothes: For most of the year lightweight, summer clothes are essential, although in the mountains a sweater will be needed in the evening. When visiting churches or monasteries, women should be modestly dressed or they will be refused admission.

Drink prices: Alcohol on the whole is cheap. Representative prices are: wine, 2s to 5s a bottle; Cyprus Brandy, 7s to 9s a bottle; Ouzo, 6s to 7s a bottle; Beer, 2s per large bottle; Scotch, 34s a bottle.

Electricity: 240 volts A.C., 50 cycles single phase. The better hotels provide 230/115 points for electric shavers.

Festivals: Folk festivals are always enjoyable and Cyprus has some very interesting ones. The order in which they are given is chronological:—

Orange Festival: Famagusta
In February the orange harvest is celebrated with displays of folk-singing and dancing and with the free distribution of oranges.
Limassol Carnival   A week of singing, dancing and processions fifty days before Easter.
May Day (Anthestiria)   All the main towns celebrate the first fortnight in May with a Flower Festival, formerly the Feast of Aphrodite. Appropriately, Paphos is probably the most colourful.
Cataclysmos   This festival, said to be a survival of the Feast of the Paphian Aphrodite Anadyomene, and later identified by the Church with Noah's survival of the Deluge and the Feast of Pentecost, takes place fifty days after Easter and adds sea games to the usual dancing and competitions. Larnaca lets itself go more than any other town on this occasion.
Folk Festival: Platres   A traditional folk festival for the hill villagers of the Troodos Mountains, this takes place at the end of August and the beginning of September.
Lemon Festivals: Lapithos
Lapithos, near Kyrenia, celebrates the citrus harvest in September.
Wine Festival: Limassol
Wine-tasting, folk-dancing, singing at the end of September to celebrate the wine harvest.
In addition to these festivals, concerts and plays are given in the summer at the following places: Salamis (restored Roman theatre), Kyrenia Castle, Bellapais Abbey, Curium (restored theatre). The local Tourist Bureaux will supply details of dates and programmes which naturally vary with the availability of actors and musicians.

Languages and Population: The population of Cyprus is 80 per cent Greek and 18 per cent Turkish, but in the towns almost everyone can speak English. Even in the remotest villages someone can usually be found to translate. Three phrasebooks that can be recommended are *Travellers' Greek* (Jonathan Cape, 6s), *Collins Greek Phrase-Book* (3s 6d) and *English-Turkish Phrasebook* (Garnstone Press, 5s).

Money: The Cyprus pound is divided into 1000 mils and is exactly equivalent to £1 sterling. Notes are in denominations of £5, £1, 500 mils and 250 mils, and there are coins of 100 mils (2s), 50 mils (1s), 25 mils (6d), 5 mils and 3 mils. Visitors may bring in an unlimited amount of sterling, provided that it is in the form of travellers' cheques, etc. Notes should not exceed £10. Overseas banks with branches in the main towns are Barclays Bank D.C.O., The Chartered Bank, the National Bank of Greece, National and Grindlays and the Türkiye is Bankasi. The leading local banks are the Bank of Cyprus and the Turkish Bank of Nicosia. Banking hours are 8 a.m. to 1 p.m. (including Saturdays).

Newspapers and Broadcasting:
The *Cyprus Mail* is published daily in English and as well as providing news also carries details of the Forces Broadcasting Service programmes which are in English. UK newspapers can usually be obtained on the day of issue. The Cyprus Broadcasting Corporation put out a number of television and radio programmes in English, as well as in Greek and Turkish.

Religion: Greek Cypriots are members of the Orthodox Church of Cyprus which is part of the Holy Orthodox Eastern Church and has a unique autocephalous status due to the miraculous discovery of the bones of St Barnabas in A.D. 477 which was regarded as proof of apostolic foundation. The Turkish Cypriot population is Sunni Muslim. There are very small minorities of Armenian Gregorians and Maronites.

Time: Cyprus time is two hours in advance of Greenwich Mean Time.

Tourist Information: The Government tourist offices are efficient and helpful. They are there to help the tourist get the best from Cyprus and will give advice on travel, local entertainment, accommodation, sightseeing and any other problem one may have.
Government Tourist Offices and Bureaux: the principal ones are:

26 Evagoras Avenue, Nicosia (Tel. 4000/2153); At Nicosia Airport (Tel. 82217); 33 Anexartisias Street, Famagusta (Tel. 4182); Opposite the Customs, Limassol (Tel. 2756); Kennedy Square, Paphos; and Demokratias Square, Larnaca (Tel. 3322). The *Cyprus Turkish Tourism Department* is located at 29 Selim II St., Nicosia.

Weights and Measures: British units of length are used, with the addition of 'pihiys' ('arshin' in Turkish) which is two feet. English weights are recognised, but the Cyprus standards are used most often. 1 dram – 0.112 oz.; 100 drams – 1 onje or onka; 400 drams – 1 oke (2.8264 lb.); English pints, quarts and gallons are used for the measurement of capacity.

BIBLIOGRAPHY

THE HISTORICAL BACKGROUND

J. Boardman, *The Greeks Overseas*, London, 1964
J. B. Bury, *A History of Greece, to the Death of Alexander the Great*, London, 1952
H. W. Catling, "Cyprus in the Neolithic and Bronze Age Periods" in *The Cambridge Ancient History*, Cambridge, 1966
V. Desborough, *The Last Mycenaeans and their Successors*, Oxford, 1964
M. Grant, *The Ancient Mediterranean*, London, 1969
F. W. Hasluck, *Christianity and Islam under the Sultans*, Oxford, 1929
P. K. Hitti, *A History of the Arabs*, London/New York, 1956
G. E. Kirk, *A Short History of the Middle East*, Washington D.C., 1949
B. Lewis, Ch. Pellat, J. Schacht (ed.), *The Encyclopaedia of Islam*, Leiden/London, 1965
Sir J. Marriott, *The Eastern Question*, Oxford, 1940
G. E. Mylonas, *Mycenae and the Mycenaean Age*, Princeton, 1966
G. Ostrogorsky, *A History of the Byzantine State*, Oxford, 1968
M. P. Price, *A History of Turkey from Empire to Republic*, London, 1956
Sir W. Ramsay, "The Intermixture of Races in Asia Minor" in *Proceedings of the British Academy*, London, 1915–16
Sir J. C. S. Runciman, *Byzantine Civilisation*, London, 1933
Sir J. C. S. Runciman, *A History of the Crusades*, Cambridge, 1953–4
S. Vryonis, *Byzantium and Europe*, London, 1967

CYPRUS IN HISTORY AND TODAY

D. Alastos, *Cyprus in History*, London, 1955
P. Balfour, *The Orphaned Realm*, London, 1951
M. Brion, *Catherine Cornaro, Reine de Chypre*, Paris, 1945
R. P. Charles, "Le peuplement de Chypre dans l'antiquité, Etude Anthropologique," in *Etudes Chypriotes II*, Paris, 1962
C. Cobham, *Excerpta Cypria*, Cambridge, 1908
A. Emilianides, *Histoire de Chypre*, Paris, 1962
C. Foley, *Island in Revolt*, London, 1962
R. Gunnis, *Historic Cyprus*, London, 1947

J. Hackett, *A History of the Orthodox Church of Cyprus*, London, 1901
C. Henderson, *Cyprus, the Country and Its People*, London, 1968
Sir G. F. Hill, *A History of Cyprus*, Cambridge, 1940–52
G. Home, *Cyprus Then and Now*, London, 1960
J. T. Hutchinson and C. Cobham, *A Handbook of Cyprus*, London, 1901, 1903, 1904, 1905
N. Iorga, *France de Chypre*, Paris, 1931
S. Kyriakides, *Cyprus: Constitutionalism and Crisis Government*, London.
Sir R. H. Lang, *Cyprus, Its History, Its Present Resources and Future Prospects*, London, 1878
de M. Latrie, *Histoire de l'Ile de Chypre sous les Lusignans*, Paris, 1852–61
Sir H. Luke, *Cyprus, a Portrait and an Appreciation*, London, 1968
Sir H. Luke, *Cyprus under the Turks*, Oxford, 1921
F-G. Maier, *Cyprus, From the Earliest Times to the Present Day* (translation from German), London, 1968
T. A. H. Mogabgab, *Supplementary Excerpts on Cyprus*, Nicosia, 1941–45
P. Newman, *A Short History of Cyprus*, London, 1953
H. D. Purcell, *Cyprus*, London, 1969
C. W. J. Orr, *Cyprus under British Rule*, London, 1918
J. Riley-Smith, "The Knights of St John in Jerusalem and Cyprus" in *A History of the Order of St John of Jerusalem*, vol. I., London, 1967
F. Sforza, *Residue di latinitá in Cipro*, Rome, 1928
C. Spyridakis, *A Brief History of Cyprus*, Nicosia, 1964
R. Stephens, *Cyprus a Place of Arms*, London, 1965
Sir R. Storrs, *A Chronology of Cyprus*, Nicosia, 1930
Sir R. Storrs and B. J. O'Brien, *The Handbook of Cyprus*, London, 1930

MEMOIRS AND DIARIES

Ali Bey-el-Abbassi, *Travels of Ali Bey in Morocco, Tripoli, Cyprus . . . etc. between the years 1803 and 1807*, London, 1816
Sir S. Baker, *Cyprus as I saw it in 1879*, London, 1879
M. Chapman, *Across Cyprus*, London, 1943
G. Grivas, *Memoirs*, London, 1964
(Lord) H. H. Kitchener, "Notes on Cyprus" in *Blackwood's Edinburgh Magazine*, Edinburgh, 1879
Mrs Lewis, *A Lady's Impressions of Cyprus*, London, 1894
W. H. Mallock, *In an Enchanted Isle*, London, 1889
Sir R. Storrs, *Orientations*, London, 1937

ARCHAEOLOGY

P. Aström, *The Middle Cypriot Bronze Age*, Lund, 1957
H. W. Catling, *Cypriot Bronzework in the Mycenaean World*, Oxford, 1964
A. P. di Cesnola, *The Lawrence Cesnola Collection*, London, 1881
L. P. di Cesnola, *Cyprus, its Ancient Cities, Tombs and Temples*, London, 1877

Bibliography

W. B. Dinsmoor, *The Architecture of Ancient Greece*, London, 1950
P. Dikaios, *A Guide to the Cyprus Museum*, Nicosia, 1961
P. Dikaios, *Khirokitia, Final Report on the Excavation of Neolithic Settlement*, London, 1953
E. Gjerstad, *Studies on Prehistoric Cyprus*, Uppsala, 1926
E. Gjerstad, *The Swedish Cyprus Expedition, Finds and Results*, Uppsala/Stockholm, 1927–56
Sir G. F. Hill, *Catalogue of Greek Coins of Cyprus*, Bologna, 1964
D. G. Hogarth, *Devia Cypria, Notes of an Archaeological Journey in Cyprus in 1888*, London, 1889
V. Karageorghis, *The Ancient Civilisation of Cyprus*, Geneva/London, 1969
V. Karageorghis, *Sculptures from Salamis*, Nicosia, 1964–66
V. Karageorghis, *Treasures in the Cyprus Museum*, Nicosia, 1962
F. A. Schaeffer, *Enkomi-Alasia, Nouvelles Missions en Chypre 1946–1950*, Paris, 1952
F. H. Stubbings, *Mycenaean Pottery from the Levant*, Cambridge, 1951
A. Westholm, *The Temples of Soli*, Stockholm, 1936
J. and S. Young, *Terracotta Figurines from Kourion in Cyprus*, Philadelphia, 1955
Recommended are issues in the series *Brief History and Description* of the important archaeological sites in Cyprus, published by the Antiquities Department

ARTS AND LITERATURE

S. Casson, *Ancient Cyprus, its Art and Archaeology*, London, 1937
The Charioteer, Nos 7 and 8. Special issue on "Cyprus, its Poetry, Prose and Art", New York, 1965
E. Esin, *Turkish Art in Cyprus*, Ankara, 1969
C. Enlard, *L'Art Gothique et la Renaissance en Chypre*, Paris, 1899
G. Jeffery, *Historic Monuments of Cyprus*, Nicosia, 1918
A. H. S. Megaw and A. Stylianou, *Cyprus Byzantine Mosaics and Frescoes* (UNESCO), New York, 1963
A. Papageorgiou, *Icons of Cyprus*, London, 1969
A. Sikelianos, *Poèmes akritiques et la mort de Digénis*, Athens, 1960
A. and J. Stylianou, *Byzantine Cyprus as Reflected in Art*, Nicosia, 1948
A. and J. Stylianou, *The Painted Churches of Cyprus*, Nicosia/London, 1964
D. Talbot Rice, *The Art of Byzantium*, London, 1959
D. Talbot Rice, R. Gunning and T. Talbot Rice, *The Icons of Cyprus*, London, 1937

MISCELLANEOUS

D. A. Bannerman, *Birds of Cyprus*, Edinburgh/London, 1958
J. K. Birge, *The Bektashi Order of Dervishes*, London, 1937
J. A. S. Bucknill, *List of the Butterflies of Cyprus*, Nicosia, 1911
Cyprus Today, Nicosia, quarterly
L. Durrell, *Bitter Lemons*, London, 1957

Sir J. G. Frazer, *The Golden Bough*, London, 1960

R. Graves, *The Greek Myths*, Harmondsworth, 1960

International Congress of Cypriot Studies, *Catalogue of Books on Cyprus from the Library of D. N. Marangos*, Nicosia, 1969

(Lord) H. H. Kitchener, *A Trigonometrical Survey of the Island of Cyprus*, London, 1885

A. Matthews, *Lilies of the Field, a Book of Cyprus Wild Flowers*, Limassol, 1968

A. J. Meyer and S. Vassiliou, *The Economy of Cyprus*, Cambridge, Mass., 1962

O. Polunin and Anthony Huxley, *Flowers of the Mediterranean*, London, 1967

W. W. Weir, *Education in Cyprus*, Nicosia, 1952

TRAVEL AND TOURISM

A. Lymbourides, *Cyprus, the Island of Aphrodite*, Nicosia, 1967

Nagel Travel Series, *Cyprus*, Geneva/Paris/Hamburg, 1966

Niyazi Babür, *English-Turkish Phrase Book*, Garnstone Press, London, 1967

R. Parker, *Aphrodite's Realm*, Nicosia, 1968

H. Thurston, *The Travellers' Guide to Cyprus*, London, 1967

B. Toy, *Rendezvous in Cyprus*, London, 1970

Travellers' Greek, London, 1963

R. Wideson, *Cyprus in Picture*, London, 1953

INDEX

Achaeans, 24, 25, 26, 59, 85, 120, 131, 145, 149
Acre, 30, 60, 138
Adonis, 26, 102, 123, 130–1
Aegisthus, 127
Aeneas, 102
Aepia, 77
Afsefthis, Theodorus, 109
Afxentiou, Gregory, 89
Afxentis, Symeon, 92
Agamemnon, 25, 126
Agapenor, 103
Agros, 88
Airport (Nicosia), 11, 52
Ajax, 145, 150
Akamas, 12, 14, 99, 114
Akhiropiitos, 72
Akrotiri, 14, 116
Alasia, 50, 149, 150
Alexander the Great, 27, 45, 77, 98, 101, 103, 113, 121, 131, 146
Alexius I Comnenus, 56
Ali Bey el Abassi (Don Domingo Badia-y-Leyblich), 34, 118
Alice, Queen, 42, 89
Amathus, 25, 27, 102, 123
Ambelia, 17, 63
Amiandos, 77, 90
Ammochostos see Famagusta
Anatolia, 24, 25, 27, 32, 45, 49, 61, 78, 98, 113, 143, 145
Ancaeus, 103
Anchises, 102
Andreas (Andrew), Cape, 12, 153
Anglo-Cypriot relations, 12, 15–17, 29–30, 34, 36–9, 61–2, 96, 116, 119, 120, 132
Animal life, 61, 98, 117–8
Anthestiria, 21
Antiphonitis, 66, 67, 151

Aphrodite (Astarte, Venus), 11, 13, 16, 21, 22, 25, 26, 27, 49, 77, 84, 100–2, 104, 105, 106, 111, 130, 133
Apollo, 23, 28, 81, 90, 105, 106, 121–2, 130, 147, 150
Apollo Hylates, Temple of, 23, 121–2
Apostolos Andreas Monastery, 153
Aqueduct of Bekir Pasha, 136
Arabs, 25, 29, 33, 41, 43, 44, 46, 56, 63, 68, 79, 105, 106, 143, 146, 152
Archaeological excavations and expeditions, 26, 47–51, 61, 73, 102, 105, 107, 121, 131, 148–150
Argates, 90
Argos *see* Achaeans, Mycenae
Ariosto, 114
Aristotle, 27
Armenian Monastery, 67
Armenians, 33, 45, 67–8, 142
Arnauti, Cape, 114
Arodaphnousa, 60
Arodhes, 107
Arsinoe, 112–13
Artemis, 90, 105
Asinou, 22, 29, 47, 70, 80–2
Asklepios, 90
Asomatos, 74
Assyria, 25, 27, 74, 121, 145
Astarte, *see* Aphrodite
Astromeritis, 80
Atatürk, 45, 55, 135
Athena, 130
Athos, Mount, 28, 108
Augustus, 27, 103
Austria, Don John of, 140
Ayia, Ayios (*see also* Saint)
Ayia Irini, 48, 73, 74–5

Index

Myrtou, 48, 74

Namik Kemal, 142
Nea Paphos, 49, 103, 104, 105–7,
 see also Palaia Paphos, Paphos
Nestorians, 33, 142
Newspapers, 16, 157
Nicocreon, 146
Nicosia, 11, 13, 14, 17, 18, 21, 22,
 30, 31, 32, 38, 40, 41–54, 60, 66,
 68, 70, 71, 79, 80, 82, 85, 89,
 97, 110, 111, 113, 127, 129, 137,
 143
Night-clubs, 52
Nikitari, 80

Olympus, Mount, 22, 74, 77, 84–7,
 98, 112, 151
Orestes, 127
Oriental impact on Cyprus, 24, 25,
 27, 33, 121, see also Anatolia,
 Assyria, Egypt, Ottoman rule,
 Persia, Phoenicians, Sumerians,
 Syria
Orpheus, 28
Orta Köy, 55
Orthodox Church, 21, 27, 28, 29,
 31, 32, 33, 35, 46, 107–11, 128,
 133–4, 136, 157
"Othello," 21, 32, 139
Ottoman rule, 17, 18, 25, 31–6, 37,
 38, 43, 60, 68, 69, 98, 105, 110,
 115, 120, 132, 135, 136, 139–
 141, 142, 145, 152
Ovid, 26, 102

Pachyammos (Karpas), 153
Pachyammos (Kyrenia), 65
Palaia Paphos, 27, 101, 102, 103,
 104, see also Paphos
Palekhori, 88
Palestine, 26
Pancyprian Exhibition, 144
Pancyprian Gymnasium, 35, 111
Pano Panayia, 111
Pano Platres, 13, 18, 21, 85–6, 87
Paphos, 17, 18, 21, 22, 25, 27, 29,
 32, 35, 68, 79, 100–13, 120, 123,
 133, 146
Paphos Museum, 104, 113
Paralimni, 144
Pasicrates, 121
Pedhieos, River, 89, 90
Pedhoulas, 85, 95, 96
Pendayia, 76
Pentadactylos, 67, 68

Pera, 90
Pericles, 27
Peristerona, 79–80
Persia, 16, 25, 27, 34, 43, 44, 45,
 48, 77, 78, 121, 131, 143, 145,
 146
Peter I, King, 60
Petra tou Dhiyeni, 106
Petra tou Limniti, 79
Petra tou Romiou, 25, 100–1, 106
Peyia, 107
Phaedra, 106
Phaliron, 65
Phanariots, 32
Phassouri, 116, 118
Philike Hetairia, 35
Phoenicians, 16, 25, 27, 90, 101,
 130, 131, 145
Pitsilia, 88–9
Platres, 13, 18, 21, 85–6, 87
Plutarch, 77, 132
Polis (tis Khrysokhous), 78, 79,
 111, 112–14
Polish Archaeological Expedition,
 50, 107
Politiko, 89–90
Polystipos, 82
Pomos, 79, 112
Portugal, 120
Prodhromos, 13, 18, 85, 95
Prometheus, 147
Ptolemies, 27, 105, 113, 121, 131,
 146
Pygmalion, 26, 102
Pyramus and Thisbe, 106

Racial composition of Cypriots, 32–
 3, 39, 53, 105, 157
Ras-el Shamra, 50, 149
Ravenna, 136
Rheims, 42, 141
Rimbaud, Arthur, 88
Rizokarpaso, 152
Rome and Roman rule, 21, 23, 25,
 27–8, 31, 48, 49, 76, 77, 90, 103,
 105, 113, 121, 131, 146–7
Rumi, Jalal-ad-din, 45
Russia, 34, 36, 81, 93, 97, 110

Saint (see also Ayia, Ayios)
St Barbara, 92
St Barnabas, 28, 79, 90, 103, 146
St Barnabas Monastery, 148
St Basil, 94
St Chrysostom, 69
St George, 92, 93
St Helena, 89, 127